GOD'S ALL STAR
BASEBALL TEAM

Art Zehr

Endorsements

Pastor Art Zehr has written an intriguing autobiography and a very insightful as well as enjoyable comparison of the baseball diamond of performance and God's diamond of grace. He writes straight from the heart with an endearing openness that will capture the heart of many a reader. It surely has captured mine!

Pastor Zehr emphasizes that interpersonal relations are of the greatest importance and that a personal relationship with Jesus is all-important. His evangelistic message is very clear: we are saved by Grace. He makes it also clear that we can only succeed in this life or the life to come by the selfless love of God. The ultimate message in this book is that without selfless love we cannot have a transformed, victorious, and abundant life.

The author presents us with a valuable, courageous and heartwarming account of one man's search for meaning and purpose in life. It is valuable because it reminds us all that every person is significant in the eyes of God and ought to be significant in our eyes as well. It is courageous because Pastor Zehr dares to be transparent in a world that seems to prefer vagueness over clarity. It is heartwarming because it reminds us that most of us, most of the time, can be overcomers in this life.

I love this book and cannot wait to give a copy of it to my dear grandson, Zachary Brandt, one of America's finest young baseball players. He too will love this book and so will his friends. And speaking of America, Pastor Zehr has done a good job by giving us a book that delivers the kind of soothing medicine that our country greatly needs.

Dr. Frans M. J. Brandt, EdD, LPC, LMFT
Author, Counselor and Psychotherapist

Here is a man not afraid to share the ups and downs of his life, ministry, and relationship with the Lord. After reading his book, not only do I know baseball a little better, I know Art, a minister under the umbrella of Mt. Zion, who has dedicated His life to demonstrating the principles of God's Kingdom on earth.

Joseph G. Milosec, Minister and author,
Mt. Zion, Clarkson, MI

Pastor Art possesses both an informal and a unique method for presenting deep spiritual concepts and precepts in a very interesting and creative manner. This book is easy to read but it is not an easy read. Like a provocative sermon, it may challenge you for days or weeks.

I consider Pastor Art, with deepest respect, to sometimes be a spiritual savant. He has many times during personal conservations revealed profound spiritual insights totally unaware. This is especially true when he prays for people and their situations. I have personally greatly benefited from his prayerful interventions.

His ministry has always been based on restoration: first to God, then to the kingdom. He always has had a special understanding and a double portion of compassion for the emotionally helpless, broken hearted and marginalized. His compassion also extends to pastors and churches who are hurting—Godly people who need a safe place to vent, reflect and pray. These are the tenants that AZ Ministries is founded upon.

This book shares his struggles and revelations from forty years of ministry. I believe you will thoroughly enjoy it.

Let me add that I have been a close personal friend of Pastor Art for over fifteen years. In our numerous conversations he has always been very respectful of the different denominations and their traditions—especially the Catholics. His view that denominational worship has its place, but that the Kingdom Church is far greater in Jesus' heart, has greatly influenced me and my theology. I can now say I am a practicing Kingdom/Catholic—in that order. Thank you, Pastor Art.

Gary Hayward
Teacher/Seeker, Flushing, MI

Why do I think my dad knows baseball?

Fact #1: He plays fantasy baseball and one year he came in 3rd in the nation out of thousands of participants. The winner makes projections of how major league players will play for the following year with the major media involved.

(continued)

Fact #2: He was my coach growing up and 100% of the players that he had coached on my teams ALWAYS stated that he was the best coach, the most fair, and most fun to play for. They stated we won a lot because of his talent in coaching and he was also able to balance winning with being fair in getting everyone with varying levels of skill and talent to play in the games.

Fact #3: I witnessed him talking to two other people at a major league game with the opponents' jerseys on. Initially, they were giving the body language they did not want to speak to him for obvious reasons. By the end of the game they were turned around, not watching the game anymore, asking him specific questions about the game of baseball. He clearly had compelled them to change their minds that relevant, accurate, and truthful knowledge can come from any source; even one that initially appears to be the opposition.

Why do I think my dad thinks outside the box?

The Bible wrote about the letter of the law in the Old Testament and the spirit of the law in the New Testament. Jesus was the perfect balance of both. As my dad has matured through life in his unique way, he has been able to achieve this understanding and been able to apply this critical balance in many outside-the-box ways, including in this baseball analogy. I am proud of his efforts, and years ago I gave him the award for MOST IMPROVED DAD. Isn't that what we are all striving for, to become the most improved we can through GOD?

Read about one man's journey in baseball, God, and life, and I guarantee it will compel you to think through how you can also improve.

Kelson Zehr, MA, LPC, LSW, CRC, CCM, CAADC, CEAP
Licensed Professional Counselor

My Dad has written a unique book that describes his personal journey through life and with God, together with a new and modern theme that relates to everyone: the baseball diamond of life. This book does not require any special knowledge or even love for the sport of baseball. Rather, it showcases the theme of the beloved sport to explore important life topics and your relationship with God.

Well known and colorful Biblical figures form God's "baseball team" and directly relate to modern character issues as we struggle to achieve grace in our walk of life. You will smile as you recall the many foibles and miraculous strengths that endear us to these historical Biblical stories and characters, and you will find yourself connecting in new ways that personally affect your life. The autobiographical background is heartfelt. The personal walk of the author, as he is at times rejecting and then welcoming the hand of God, explores how we should embrace our past mistakes and triumphs on the field of life.

Read this book and you will be reminded of the simple connection with God that must be the foundation for your faith. The tone is enthusiastic and supports what many of us have forgotten or never learned: That our walk with God is to be a walk of joy; not a task or duty, and not solely conditioned by church communities, but rather, by the strength and commitment that comes first from a direct relationship with God. Many facets of our life (especially sports and other hobbies) are topics that are never connected to God as we tend to compartmentalize our lives. This book renews the meaningful interconnection of applying your faith to all topics of life (including the fun stuff!) and the strength of character that only comes from human "errors" and circling back to what we knew in the first place but have perhaps misplaced: The joy of a relationship with God is easy and is in fact a choice.

Starla D. Zehr, Attorney-at-Law

Published by

Olive Press צהר זית
Messianic and Christian Publisher

P.O. Box 163
Copenhagen, NY 13626

Messianic & Christian Publisher

Our prayer at Olive Press is that we may help make the Word of Adonai fully known, that it spread rapidly and be glorified everywhere. We hope our books help open people's eyes so they will turn from darkness to Light and from the power of the adversary to God and to trust in ישׁוע Yeshua (Jesus). (From II Thess. 3:1; Col. 1:25; Acts 26:18,15 NRSV and CJB, the *Complete Jewish Bible*) May this book in particular help draw men to answer God's call to them.

In honor to God, pronouns referring to the Trinity are capitalized, satan's names are not. But not all Bible versions do this and legally must be printed as they are.

www.olivepresspublisher.com

Cover and interior design by Olive Press Publisher.
Cover photos of baseballs © 2012 by Allan Miller.
Photos of the little boys on cover and on pp. 130-31 © 2012 by Gary Hayward.
Photos on p. 151 © 2012 by Karen Eddy
All other photos and images are the property of the author.

GOD'S ALLSTAR BASEBALL TEAM

ISBN 978-0-9855241-5-9   Printed in the USA.
1. Christian Inspirational 2. Christian Spiritual Growth 3. Christian-Charismatic

All Scriptures, unless otherwise indicated, are taken from the *New King James Version*. Copyright © 1982 by Thomas Nelson, Inc. All rights reserved.

Scriptures marked:

NIV are taken from the *Holy Bible, New International Version*. Copyright © 1973, 1978, 1984 by International Bible Society. All rights reserved.

KJV are taken from the *King James Version* of the Bible.

NRSV are taken from the New Revised Standard Version of the Bible, copyright © 1989 National Council of the Churches of Christ in the USA. Used by permission. All rights reserved.

NLT are taken from the The Holy Bible, New Living Translation. Copyright © 1996, by Tyndale House Publishers, Inc., Wheaton, IL 60189 USA. All rights reserved.

This book is dedicated to my family, friends, and mentors, and those whom I have mentored.

Acknowledgments:

I want to thank everyone who has encouraged me in obeying God by heading to my "Nineveh"—writing this book! These people include my good friend, Gary Hayward and his wife and sons, my wonderful friend and mentor Dr. Frans M. J. Brandt. It includes my kids Starla and Kelson (on the front cover at bat), my pastor Loren Covarrubias and his wife Bonnie and all my friends at Mt. Zion Church. It also includes my dad who is pictured on the front cover at 90 years old. He's the one who introduced me to baseball and he will be the first to receive a copy of this book.

I would also like to thank my editor/publisher, Cheryl Zehr. I was sold (and my board was too when I told them later) when she said, "I try not to change the author's voice. I depend on God's inspiration and direction. I make sure the author agrees on everything, and we leave all in God's timing." She was clearly not motivated by money. I felt comfortable telling her about my weakest points in life for this book. I saw the spirit of Olive Press writings. It was not a religious spirit, but the Holy Spirit.

Finally and most sincerely, I thank the Holy Spirit for His revelation. To God be the glory!

Foreword:

This book is written to share the Good News of Jesus Christ (the diamond of Life) and to encourage and support others in their faith walk in following the Holy Spirit, and to equip saints with an understanding of their ministry and release them into fruitful function.

The Holy Spirit is calling the church to prepare and make ready. If we judge ourselves, we will not be judged, but if we hide sin in our hearts and cling to what is wrong, judgment will come to us.

When we fail, if we turn to the Lord, He is merciful. One appointed Sunday evening in 1987 I had an overwhelming spiritual experience. God let me know that my failure had not spoiled His divine plan. My spark that was almost out was re-ignited by the Holy Spirit into a fire that cannot be quenched. Now I live "saved by grace, justified by faith, sanctified by mercy, surrounded by love, endowed with power from on high, encouraged by the community of saints, and kept safely in the palm of God's hand!" [Dr. Frans M. J. Brandt, *The Renewed Mind*, p. 21, copyright 1982,1984,1999, WinePress Publishing, P.O. Box 428, Enumclaw, WA 98022.]

JESUS certainly did not die for us so we could be joyless and miserable. He actually said in John 10:10 that He came so we could have life and enjoy it. Imagine that! Jesus wants us to enjoy life! I pray this book will be a HOME RUN for you and that you become inspired by GOD with the joy of the LORD in the power of the HOLY SPIRIT. Let's spread the GOOD NEWS THAT SERVING JESUS IS A JOYFUL THING!

I know this baseball analogy
is not the answer for everything.
Only Jesus
the Truth, the Way, and the Life
is the complete answer for everything.

Contents

Foreward: 11

Chapter 1 Chosen   15

Chapter 2 Called   29

Chapter 3 Commissioned   57

Chapter 4 Relaunched   107

Me at eight months, not able to sit up yet due to being born premature.

Me a hefty 26 llbs. at age one.

Chapter 1

Chosen

"God, <u>WHAT</u> is the bottom line here?"
"<u>WHERE</u> , Savior, can I find Your Spirit and attitude in this?"
"Lord, teach me <u>HOW</u> to perceive, understand, and apply Your
* Heart in my part of Your eternal purposes."*
"<u>WHEN</u>?" Now!
Get on your mark, get set, <u>GO</u>!!!!

*T*he race of life started for me at 4:21 pm on July 28, 1944 in Lowville, New York. I was the first son of three to Floyd and Laura Zehr. I came early (over a month), and weighed in at 4 pounds 13 ounces!

The first question my dad asked was, "Will he make it?" You see, my mother had trouble getting pregnant. One of her sisters was also not able to conceive, so my mother assumed this was true for her. Then she did get pregnant but had a miscarriage. So the whole time she was carrying me, they wondered if they would lose me. Then I came early and tiny. So now you see why my father asked if I would make it. He has asked that question many times since, and as I write this book in his 92nd year, he probably is still asking that question!

What a celebration party they gave me! What attention and affirmation! Everybody was praying in faith and hope, believing I would make it. Would my lungs be okay? Would I be able to talk?

Mom exclaimed to me years later, "Your dad told you to 'Grow up!' and you did! You went from four pounds to 26 pounds in just one year!"

[Our heavenly father also says to us, "Grow up! Mature in the faith!" Will we listen to Him? We will address how to become mature sons later. For now let's get back to the story.]

When the trouble was over—the storm past—when there were no more worries about my health and after a couple brothers came along, I found out the party was also over! There was little attention—little affirmation, and I was allowed to talk only a little.

I ran everywhere looking for someone to talk to. Some would give me a few minutes and then come up with different excuses to try to stop me most times. Everybody seemed too busy to meet my main need: <u>a listening ear</u> to fill my loneliness. I began to think, "Maybe I am not that important." I didn't know who I was or if I belonged, or if I would make it.

I did find one person that gave me the time of day. It was my neighbor, Nevin. My dad and mom said we could never have had better neighbors than Nevin Lehman and his wife, Donna. He had been my dad's boss while also being the neighborhood barber out of his home part-time. By the time I was eight years old, he was a barber full-time in the barber shop at his house, and he was also my bus driver. He had a small barn behind his barber shop. His barn had only one door. Nevi always had time for me. I appreciated his attention and affirmation. We were always bantering and kidding. Being a runner, I was always telling him, "You can't catch me!" He would chase me, but I always got away.

One day in his barn, he told me, "If you say that one more time, I will catch you and throw you into the pigpen." I didn't listen to him because I was sure I could outrun him. But I didn't realize that he had locked the barn door. So he caught me and lifted me up to pretend to throw me into the pigpen. I wrestled him as he was lifting me in the air. This threw him off balance which caused him to lose his hold on me and into the pigpen I went! What a mess! Mom would not like this!!

GOOD NEIGHBORS - Art and Carlton Zehr, sons of Floyd Zehr of Croghan, visit with their neighbor, Nevin Lehman (right) and his dog. Floyd says the Zehrs and the Lehmans were good friends and good neighbors. The snapshot was taken about the spring of 1950.

Mom was my hero. I thought the world of her, and I always wanted to please her. Bringing pigpen filth into the house would definitely not help with that! I didn't want to have to explain it to her. I wanted to be perfect in her eyes.

I KNEW I had crossed the line. Which part of Nevin's "no" had I not understood? I knew I was in the wrong spirit and attitude. I had perceived, understood, and applied my thoughts and feelings wrongly. God was using Nevin for His eternal purposes. Would I get my part right? No, not yet. I was not ready to change.

I didn't blame Nevin. I blamed myself. I couldn't lie to Mom, but I prayed she would never know. I came in by the back door of the house and made sure I washed out my clothes myself so she wouldn't find out. Nevi (his nickname that I used in casual moments) and I had made a pact that my mom would never hear of it. I actually never did come totally clean with her about it. I wanted affirmation so badly that I couldn't take the

17

risk of letting this poor performance be known. I overly wanted to please Mom who represented the "church" to me.

I was in the race of life, the diamond of performance. I tried so hard to be perfect and to not fail! This didn't bring me much joy!

*M*y mother, coming from a large family, learned to be a hard worker. She was number six of thirteen children—a baker's dozen! Her parents were very caring, nurturing people who took care of others besides their own thirteen kids. When the children were older and leaving home, my grandmother took care of the elderly in her home. They sold the farm and bought a big house where she cared for up to six people at a time.

To show you a little of what a wonderful person my mom was, here is a prayer she embroidered on one of her special dish towels.

A Kitchen Prayer

Bless my little kitchen, Lord
I love its very look
And guide me as I do my best
Especially when I cook.

May the food I prepare
Be seasoned from above
With thy blessing and thy grace
But most of all thy love.

So bless my little kitchen, Lord
And those who share my bread
Bless its homey atmosphere
And all those I have fed.

My mother had a tremendous work ethic. She worked outside the home doing professional cleaning for a lot of professionals, people well-respected in the community. They would ask for her specifically and she picked which ones she would work for. Later

on, people asked her to teach them how to drive. (This was before driver's ed, of course.) All total, she gave driving lessons to a lot of people in the community so they could get their license.

So you see, Mom was very particular about things. And coming from a large family, she didn't miss a thing. That's why I couldn't get away with much. And do you think I never tried? No wonder I had to go to people like Nevi, because "you couldn't get away with nothing" around Mom!

*T*here were some special times to look forward to in my life. My father, nicknamed Samsie, was a good ball player and a great, successful manager. As a family we spent a lot of time at the ball field. At games, there was a lot of party celebration, along with affirmation, joyfulness, and praise. The cars even honked their horns at the great hits and field plays. And people would go wild when we won, which happened often! If someone struck out or made a bad play, the crowd would encourage or support them anyway! As a young child I always wondered why there was more celebration, affirmation, encouragement, and support on the ball field than in the church.

Sometimes the realities of life are tough. We develop all kinds of ways to escape, to not have to think about our situation. I escaped my unmet need for attention and affirmation by developing and honing a fantasy of becoming a great ball player. I practiced pitching against the garage for hours, throwing much harder when Nevi's wife Donna was playing the piano. I would also run and run and run. I was still the skinny kid that most wondered if I would make it. I even wondered myself. I gave myself no grace. I was on the wrong diamond of Life.

The bantering fun with Nevi continued as I grew older. I loved to run. Our high school had no track, but because of Nevi's good nature I found an outlet for running. The school was about

19

a mile from my house. Most mornings when the snow wasn't too deep, I would race Nevi's bus to school, all in fun. My house was his last stop, but there were two stop signs, two railroad track crossings, and one stoplight at the main road between our house and the school. When Nevi stopped the bus at the neighbor's house, I would yell out the challenge, "I'll beat you to school!" He would laugh as he revved up his engine to take me on. With the bus full of students cheering me on, I would dart off running beside the bus.

As I turned at the tracks for a short cut straight to school, I would hear the yells out the bus windows, "Go, Art. Go!" I usually won the race to the delight of the kids and to the fun teasing of Nevi.

Nevi was like an Enoch to me. He was a Godly man, respected in the community as a man of integrity and character, and he had time for me! He wanted me to be part of the team.

My father was a very busy, successful man. He was the foreman of a large paper mill, JP Lewis Company in Beaver Falls, NY. He worked there from 1951 to 1983. The last five years he was the scaler, measuring all the pulp. JP Lewis said, "Floyd, you go out there and give honest measurements. Don't beat nobody, so they keep coming in here." It worked. People soon learned that Floyd gave an honest scale and soon they were swamped with business. Customers even brought him ice cream in thanks.

In 2004, Dad wrote the following article for the church newsletter about his first "job" as a young boy.

My First Job
By Floyd Zehr

In the last part of May 1932 during the Great Depression on a Friday night, my Uncle and Aunt Emmanuel Lehman and Christina Lehman came over to Beaver Falls on the Second Road to visit my parents, Christian and Martha Zehr.

In those days, most all farm work was done with horses. I just loved to drive horses and my uncle Emmanuel Lehman knew that. That was the reason he came over. He asked my parents if I could go home with them and drive his second team of horses Saturday on the ridge Road toward Dadville. This was a milk station that took in milk in station cans. It was called Swamp Station.

At this time of year there was a surplus, more than they could process and that had to be hauled to Castorland to the big milk station there.

It was transported in high iron wheel wagons with a big seat up front. A big wagon would hold possibly 36 station cans, 3 cans wide and 12 cans deep.

My uncle had to haul between 60 and 70 cans on Saturday and needed a driver for his second team.

My parents agreed to let me go and help him out.

My uncle had two good pairs of horses, a young, frisky pair and an old, gentle pair. My uncle gave me a choice on Saturday morning of which pair I wanted to drive. I chose the old, gentle pair.

Saturday morning right after breakfast we started for Swamp Station. We loaded my uncle's wagon first, a full load of 36 station cans. The team I drove had the rest of the station cans, another 32 cans, and then we set out for Castorland, NY.

We arrived there approximately a few minutes before 9 a.m. and the men at the plant asked my uncle who his new driver was. My uncle replied, "That is my nephew, Floyd Zehr, from Beaver Falls, NY."

I didn't have to help unload the cans, the men did all the work. I sat in the big seat up front and watched. When empty I drove away and waited for my uncle as he picked up the paper work to show he delivered two loads.

It sure was a day of learning many new things, but the biggest surprise I got is when my Aunt Christian tucked me in Saturday night. She gave me a brand new, shiny dime.

I said, "I don't need any money. I just loved to drive horses."

"No," she said, "this is your wages for the good job you did today."

It was one of the best days I ever had visiting other people and driving a pair of good horses which would have followed the first team to Castorland without a driver.

As I said, Dad's nickname is Samsie. Some people only know him by that name. Here's how he tells the story today at the age of 93 of how he acquired that name.

"On my first day of school, Mom told me to go over to Harold Noftsier's house and walk with him. He was 3-4 years older than me. She told me, 'Go early so he doesn't have to wait for you.'

"I did that and he took me to school. But he didn't take me inside. Instead he had me stay outside and wrestle with the other boys. I was taking them down. Soon the others all started yelling, 'Take him, Samson! Take him!' I worked hard on the farm and I was able to wrestle all of them down, even the older boys. So, I got that nickname before I ever went into the school. At that time they were saying the whole name Samson. Later it got shortened to Samsie."

Dad was also known to the community as the baler man. He owned three baler machines. He fixed farmer's balers for them and custom baled hay for those who needed it done.

HAPPY 85TH FLOYD
TO A GOOD FRIEND

By Frank Hanno on 8/27/04

If your baler needs repair
Don't throw your arms up in despair.
No need to call those equipment dealers
Those guys are all checkbook stealers.

Just call 346-1265
Yes, folks, Floyd Zehr will soon arrive.
When you see that red Jeep coming
You can bet that baler will soon be humming.

He doesn't come to second guess
Nor does he give you a lot of jest.
When he gets working there is no doubt
He knows those balers inside and out.

For many years he's been around
But it doesn't seem to slow him down.
He's probably forgotten more than most guys know
About how to get those balers to go.

Let's hope the Lord gives him many more years
That will eliminate our baler fears.
Good baler men are hard to find
And Floyd Zehr won't charge you blind.

One day Dad took me along to his uncle, Menno Moser's farm, which is now the Mennonite Heritage Farm. Menno was a successful dairy farmer who also had about thirty sheep. While Dad was working on Menno's baler, Menno took me along with

him to help with his evening chores. He asked me to call the sheep for him. I was about eight years old. I called and called, but got no response from the sheep. So Menno called and they came running to the barn to be fed and protected for the night. He checked each one individually and told me their names, their spirit and attitude and why some were better followers and others were leaders. He knew his sheep and I could tell they knew him. I had called and called for them but they wouldn't come for me. They didn't belong to me. They belonged to him. They loved him and he loved them. They had a relationship with him. They belonged to him. Menno was like David in the Bible. He sang and played for his sheep.

Menno was mentoring me to understand that God wanted me to be like his sheep—to hear and follow His voice; not to hear any other or follow any other voice. God wanted me to know that He would take care of me as Menno did his sheep. The Spirit of God planted seeds of Truth that day in my life. I didn't understand the principles that day about me being a sheep and trusting my Master. The only thing I understood that day was I wanted something to belong to me, that would listen to my voice while I fed it. I made this wish known to my dad. Soon afterward he bought me my first calf.

My first calf.

𝓜y second mentor Andrew Moser was a man of God that listened and followed God. He was a man that had "time" for you and was friendly. He was one of the first people in my life who didn't try to change me. He believed in me and thought I was special. He said, "I have never seen anybody with more energy than you." He believed God gave me that energy. He thought that someday I would be a minister because I loved people and animals. I was outgoing and friendly and was good at remembering names. He said that people like to see that in a minister. He also said his son, Elmer, would become a minister, which came true. I liked being around Andrew. He gave me freedom and respect. He liked how I was wired.

Andrew had a farm as did most of the men in my neighborhood and in my church. There were a lot of cats on his farm and they really liked Andrew. I wanted them to like me too. As I got older, I helped Andrew with haymaking. He drove the tractor. I stacked the bales of hay on the wagon as the baler machine spit them out. As the baler lifted up the rows of piled hay from the ground, it always uncovered many a mouse that had been hiding under there. Whenever I saw a field mouse racing away, I would jump off the wagon and catch it. Being a fast runner, I was usually successful and usually got back on the wagon in time to catch the next bale of hay and stack it. I put the dead mice in a container where extra twine was kept. By the time we got back to the barn in the evening, I would have ten or more mice to offer to the cats. Those cats soon began to like me because I brought them food.

Most people didn't like how I was wired, but Andrew told me God created, called, and chose me that way for His Team! I started to believe that maybe God did have a plan and purpose for me. I longed for God's "Atta boy!"

Andrew was like an Abel to me as he imparted truths. One example was telling me, "Art, you are fun to be with. You like to

laugh and get others to laugh." Andrew has passed away and never realized what an impact he had on my life.

Laughter can be a witness in many ways. We have been misled if we have come to think of laughter and fun as being carnal or even questionable as was taught in some churches when I was young. This is one of Satan's sharpest darts, and from the looks of some of our faces, we have been punctured too many times. Looking stern and severe is nothing new. The frowning sour sect got started in the first century. Its members were a scowling band of religious stuffed shirts called Pharisees. Jesus' strongest words were directed at them. Their super serious, ritually rigid lifestyle angered our Lord!

Charles Spurgeon was the famous preacher of London. He could have easily allowed himself to become a sober, stoop-shouldered pastor who carried the weight of London around on his back. But he was a real character! He dearly loved life. His favorite sound was laughter and frequently he leaned back in the pulpit and roared with laughter over something that struck him funny. He infected people with cheer germs. Those who caught this disease found their load lighter and their Christianity brighter!

Andrew told me I was winsome. What is winsomeness? It is that appealing magnetic quality—that charisma—the ability to cause joy and genuine pleasure in the thick of it all. When a coach has it, the team shows it. Our owner, general manager, and manager have it. They want us to have fun playing ball.

Whether it is true or not that I am winsome, it is something I aspire to be. Why? Because winsomeness motivates. It releases the stranglehold grip of the daily grind. It takes the sting out of reality. Winsomeness simplifies. Things suddenly become less complicated, less severe, less bothersome. Winsomeness encourages without ignoring the wrong. It focuses on the benefits, the hope, the answers (Proverbs 17:22, I Thessalonians 5:5-16).

I was good at running and at pitching for baseball (and talking and laughing), but when it came to things like fixing machines or building things, I was no good. My dad was a genius at fixing machines. The local tractor company would even call him in when they had a tough case. My brothers are great handy-men like him. I have no such skills. Even today, my brothers still say, "If you need something done, hire someone else to do it, just to save your life."

My good friend, John Young, a pastor, counselor, and electrician agrees whole heartedly with my brothers. He knows me well. In fact, he goes a step further and tells me he will come and do the work himself just to save my life. He has called me from across America, after he moved to other states, asking me, "Art, do you have someone who can help you?" He doesn't think I'm dumb, he just thinks I'm stupid when it comes to electricity and such. He told me one time when I was younger that there are three different voltages of electricity: 110, 220, and 440. I asked him how one could tell the difference. He answered tongue in cheek, knowing I was ignorant and gullible, "You take off your shoes and socks and put your feet in water and your finger in a socket. If your fingers curl, it's 110. If your hands curl, it's 220. If everything curls, it's 440." I chose not to try his electricity test. I knew it was all in fun. Even though he was teasing, I could still feel his respect for me. Years later he had me do counseling with him for some people in his ministry.

My high school graduation picture.
I was lean and mean then. I'm no
longer lean. but ...

Chapter 2

Called

*A*t fourteen, after hearing evangelist Myron Augsburger preach, I went forward and accepted Jesus as my Savior. I was later baptized and joined the Lowville-Croghan Conservative Mennonite Church. It was the bishop of that church, Richard Zehr, who went over the plan of salvation with me when I went forward.

At seventeen, I attended an evangelistic crusade meeting conducted by Myron Augsburger, so I heard him preach again. There I submitted to the Lordship of Jesus Christ. At that point Christianity became a deeper personal commitment for me.

Two evenings later, I felt the Holy Spirit calling me to a unique ministry comprised of some of the same elements I had witnessed in Myron Augsburger's services. The next evening he asked me to share my testimony at that meeting.

College and Volunteer Service

Chosen before the foundation of the earth, created, re-created, and now called, I went for two years of Bible study to Eastern Mennonite College in Harrisonburg, Virginia from 1962-1964, where Myron Augsburger was college president. I greatly admired that man. He was one of my main first spiritual mentors and role models. I wanted to be like him. He was like an Abraham to me—a spiritual father. Under his leadership, I was taught by Christ's Spirit and formed by Christ's mind. *I will pray with the spirit but I will pray with the mind also. I will sing praise with the spirit but I will sing praise with the mind also* (I Cor. 14:15).

I got very involved in church work in the Harrisonburg community which included preaching, teaching, and especially evangelism.

I wanted to be on the baseball team. The coach told me that I would help the team best by playing short stop and batting second. I had never done either. His short stop had just graduated and he already had strong players in the other positions. He asked me, "Art, are you willing to do what is best for the team?" I didn't want to bat second. I had a strong arm. I was used to hitting home runs. He was wanting me to hit the opposite way. I wrestled with this in myself, but I wanted to be on the team so badly that I agreed to it. I had to learn to bunt and to hit the ball the other way behind the runner if there was one on base. The coach took me to another level in batting. I eventually learned to hit with more power the other way. I needed to make some serious changes. I had to use more power in running to get on base and less power in hitting. It really helped me become a more mature player. I ended up being a starter on the team for every game my whole time in college.

I also had the chance to run, run, run. I became a championship runner never losing a cross country competition while in college. Wow! God was having fruitfulness come out from all my hard work at home! I rejoiced that I had continued to press on to be an overcomer.

I did sixteen months of volunteer work in Colorado as part of the two years required by the government for my CO (Conscientious Objection) service. While there, I did the Pikes Peak 26.8 mile marathon on a trail up and down the mountain. I finished it in 6 hours and 20 minutes.

God also blessed me in shooting a special buck. My family was coming to visit and I knew my two brothers and Dad wanted to go hunting. I prayed that God would provide and reveal His

presence and give us special memories. My dad heard of a guy more than a hundred miles away from where I lived who had hunting land. I couldn't believe Dad was willing to sacrifice to travel further to hunt. We ended up hunting only ten minutes and got three deer.

We were driving along the road. There wasn't much woods. My brother Francis said, "There's not a deer within 41 miles of here. Why are we going hunting?"

Dad said, "There's one right there!" We looked and sure enough there *was* one right beside the road. We got out. Carlton went into the woods and shot it. Another one jumped out and Carlton got that one also. I went on down the hill to look and one came right out of the little woods right at me, just a stone's throw away. I quickly raised my gun—didn't even have time to aim and shot him. He went running off. I took off in the opposite direction and met him at the bottom of the hill. I was about to shoot when he went down. So, I laid my gun down and grabbed hold of his antlers to start dragging him. It's a good thing I grabbed with both hands because he wasn't dead yet, and he threw me ten feet! I grabbed my gun but he took one last breath and died, so I didn't shoot him again, but I waited awhile before I touched him this time! As you will learn later, this wasn't to be my last run-in with a deer.

That deer, I was told, was the second largest one killed that year in that area of Colorado. It was an eight pointer with a 25 ½ inch inside spread. God answered my prayers above and beyond what I prayed in believing faith.

The buck I shot in Colorado.

My Brothers

Let me tell you about my two brothers. To tell you about them, I first have to tell you a little more about Mom. As I mentioned before, Mom taught 30-35 people in the community how to drive. They all passed their driving test to get their license, except one. There was one professional lady who had a lot of anxiety whenever she was taking the test and couldn't pass it. Mom thought that this lady needed to learn to associate driving with fun. So she decided to have the lady drive her to Watertown, about an hour away, once a week to go shopping together. My dad was a little surprised at this. He asked Mom, "Laura, do you need any money?"

Her quick response was, "No, I don't. I've got money that ain't never been spent!" Mom's idea worked. After a few weeks, the lady was able to pass the state driving test.

Well, since Mom was so successful as a driving teacher, I always wondered why she suddenly quit. So one day when I asked her, "Mom, why did you quit when it was so much fun for you?"

"Well, the Bible says that a prophet is not without honor except in his hometown. Everything was fine until it was time to teach your brother, Carlton. You had trouble with boundaries, Art. But Carlton believed that no one should give him rules or laws. He just made them up as he went along. And you know, Carlton had been driving tractor since he was nine years old. He didn't think he needed his mom's help to learn to drive.

"I only had one person who was scared in the car. I took her shopping to Watertown to get her over that fear. I wasn't just going for the shopping like you might have thought. But with Carlton, it wasn't him who was scared, I was scared to ride with him!"

Now I was curious. "How did Francis do, Mom?" I asked.

"Francis?! He thought he owned the road and he thought his place was in the middle! Now you know why I quit teaching driving lessons!"

Just recently, I was talking to Carlton. I said, "I'm glad Mom told me about you and Francis. I always thought I was her favorite. Now I know! (Until I have my next problem.)" We laughed together, reminiscing about Mom.

Now I must tell you a story Dad recently told me about Francis. It happened on Halloween. Francis, who since became a politician, was honing his government and people management skills with Dad's brand new, black car. He went to Marilley E. M. Co. Hardware store in Croghan and bought several dozen eggs. Then he conscripted a couple friends. One was right-handed; one left-handed. This way he had the best leverage. In the dark of that Halloween night, he drove Dad's shiny, new car up and down the small town streets and the three of them hit anything that moved with those eggs.

This was the height of fun to three sixteen-year-old guys. The only problem was things started to come flying back in their direction, hitting Dad's new car.

33

Well, Francis got home late that night, tired. So he parked the car out of sight in the garage where Dad wouldn't see it as Dad drove the old car to work. The new car was for Mom to use and the next day wasn't a day she would use it. So, the next morning he went to school and planned to clean it after school. When he came home and went to the garage, water bucket and rag in hand, he couldn't believe what he saw. The black car was now red! It had been hit by too many tomatoes. The mess was now baked on. Soapy water was not very affective in removing it.

Dad came home before the problem was solved. Carlton and I were sure we'd lost our baby brother. Francis was definitely not Mom and Dad's favorite child right then!

Francis said, "Well, Dad, everybody was just throwing tomatoes at my car. We just drove back and forth waving and they just threw things at us."

Dad tells me today, "My car looked like WWI, II, and III!! It took hours to take all the stuff off. I didn't think it would ever look new again. I was so mad and I got madder and madder as we were cleaning. "

Francis says, "I knew it got hit a few times. But I couldn't even tell what color the car was! It was tomatoes and who knows what all else!"

Well, Dad says after a few days, he finally got himself calmed down from it. Then later he stopped to buy something at Marilley's. "Hey, Samsie," Marilley greeted him. "What's going on down at your place?"

"Oh, not much."

"Well, I was just wondering because your son was in here the other night and he bought me out of eggs!"

"Oh." Suddenly Dad knew that the attacks on his car weren't unprovoked. His blood began to boil again.

"What did he want all those eggs for anyway?"

Dad tried to stay calm, "Well," he paused searching for what to say. "It wasn't for cooking purposes."

"Well, I had almost thirty dozen. Shoulda been plenty. Then he and a couple friends came in and bought me out!" Marilly told him. Thirty dozen eggs! Dad was getting madder by the minute. He had to get out of there fast.

On another day, after Marilley figured things out, he jokingly teased Dad. "I found out those eggs didn't all get delivered to your house. I hope they aren't the eggs that got delivered all over Croghan!"

As I said, Francis grew up to be a politician. He moved to Virginia and became the youngest person in his county to be in charge of the roads. When heard this, I said, "Mom, do you understand now his calling—why he always drove in the middle of the road? Now he is in charge of the roads where he lives in Virginia."

"He's in charge of the roads!?" she exclaimed. "Is it safe to go to Virginia?"

Francis went on to become a teacher. He is now running for the board of education. It's a good thing it is in Virginia because I don't know how many votes he would get in Croghan. He will do well as a board member. At age 16, he already knew how to solve all the problems in a small community: Shoot at anything that moves!

Dad says, "I couldn't laugh about it for a long time. But eventually, I learned to see the humor in it."

If there is something that embarrasses us too much or causes us too much pain, we need to talk to God about it and to someone we trust so we can be healed. We need to choose the right person to talk to about it. The discussion needs to lead to healing and resolution, not to escalating arguing and hard feelings. The conversation needs to help bring us to the Lord for healing.

Now let me tell you a little bit more about Carlton. One Christmas we bought him a plaque that described exactly how he lives. He quotes it often. It says, "Life doesn't begin at 40 for those who went like 60 (mph) at 20 (years old)." Another favorite saying of Carlton is, "Sleep is a habit. You can do it after you die."

Most people would say that if someone has no high school education, they're not going to get very far in life. Carlton and I would agree. However, Carlton never went to high school himself. But he had a tremendous work ethic which he learned from Mom and Dad. He always started working before 6 am. God blessed him with money-making skills. Today, he is a very successful businessman. God has blessed him financially, unbelievably. Most people would be jealous of the money he has.

He has two Dodge Vipers. One day he asked me if I wanted to ride in one of his Vipers. I said, "Sure, I'm a man of faith." I eagerly joined him in the two seat sports car. I didn't know what I was in for. This man of faith learned to pray a lot better on that trip!

This is a high-powered hot rod. He took me in it to see a neighbor. It didn't take long to get there. He wasn't home. Carlton said, "That's okay, he'll know I was here. I'll leave him my calling card." He left something alright.

It was always Carlton's fantasy in life to be a Nascar driver. He was fulfilling his dream. He made a pit stop at his neighbor's and then left his mark in rubber on his driveway. His neighbor definitely found out he was there!

Riding in my brother's Viper.

I was asked one time if it bothered me that he has more money than I do. I said, "Sometimes I have some questions wondering why he has a lot more than I when he doesn't go to church and I do. Then I realized that God could probably trust him more than me because he gives to the poor. That's one thing he has always been good at."

The government could learn a lot from Carlton: Work hard. Give people second chances, but don't enable them. And always leave a "calling card."

You know, God left us His calling card. He gave us Jesus, so that we can know that God cares about us.

More Volunteer Service

After that successful hunting experience with my dad and brothers while I lived in Colorado, I continued my volunteer service eight months longer in Kansas at the Kansas City Teen Center.

Kansas City Teen-Center. Pictured, from left, Betty Bethel, VS-er Arthur Zehr, Russell Yoder, and VS Administrator Ken Seitz.

Volunteering at the Kansas City Teen Center.

The article says, "VS-er, Arthur Zehr, is assisting the Stutzmans in supervising the center. Staff members will do referral counseling and attempt to relate the youth to the church."

In my volunteer service I learned a couple important things. I learned to serve others and I learned not to gossip.

TOWN GOSSIP

Source unknown

Sarah, the church gossip and self-appointed supervisor of the church's morals, kept sticking her nose into other people's business. Several residents were unappreciative of her activities, but feared her enough to maintain their silence.

She made a mistake, however, when she accused George, a new member, of being an alcoholic after she saw his pickup truck parked in front of the town's only bar one afternoon.

She commented to George and others that everyone seeing it there would know that he was an alcoholic. George, a man of few words, stared at her for a moment and just walked away. He said nothing.

Later that evening, George quietly parked his pickup in front of Sarah's house.

AND he left it there all night.

Marriage and Ministry

When I finished my two years of service, I married a gal I met in college. We lived in her community for four years. The highlights were two children born to us, Starla and Kelson.

We enjoyed being in charge of the youth at church. They were very successful in Bible quizzing! My wife was a nurse and a very good mother. She was also an excellent singer and appreciated music.

One day Kelson asked his mother to ask me for my blessing for him to be a saxophone player. At first I was not open. I wanted my "only son" to be a sportsman. But Mother didn't let up, and now I'm very glad she didn't. She was right and I was wrong. I am

so proud of my son. He is a great counselor and a great sportsman, but best of all, he is a man God uses in a special anointing on the sax!

He asked for his father's blessing and got it from his Heavenly Father, then finally from me.

The photo above of Kelson with his new sax looks worn because I have carried it in my wallet all these years. You know our Heavenly Father delights in us and loves you much more than I love Kelson. If He had a pocket, He would be carrying your photo in it too.

ALBION COLLEGE
"Commencement Ceremony"
May 9, 1992

Starla Dawn Zehr graduated June 2 with honors from Oakland University, Rochester, earning a bachelor's degree. Zehr was on the dean's list throughout her college career. She will be attending Wayne State University's Law School this fall.

Starla Dawn Zehr graduated from Wayne State University Law School on May 15. She received awards from the Arthur Neef Moot Court competition and the Donald E. Barris trial competition in which she placed first in the winter of 1994 and runner-up in the fall of 1993. She passed the July bar exam and became a member of the state bar on Nov. 16 She is currently practicing law in Oakland County and is an associate with A. Lawrence Russell & Associates, P.C.

Zehr

My beautiful daughter, Starla, who is a very successful attorney and counselor-at-law, came to me asking that I pray a prayer of blessing over her for a husband. I do not remember all that I prayed. But I do remember asking God in Jesus' Name by His Spirit's power to bring someone with great eyesight who would love her deeply and would see and appreciate her beauty like God and I did!

Duane is an engineer. Can you believe it? A lawyer and an engineer married, spending their lives together?! But he is a man that deeply loves her. He also has special eyesight. He is a special marksman in shooting due to his great vision! God answers our prayers!

*A*s a family we were called to Lockport Mennonite Church in Stryker, Ohio for the year of 1971. They voted me in as a licensed pastor. At the end of the year there was to be another vote for the congregation to decide whether to keep me on and ordain me. I was delighted. It was the best year so far of my life. I felt like I was

doing exactly what I had been created, called, and chosen to be and do for God. I was sold out for God and the church. My ministry was going very well, but I didn't realize the toll my zeal, long hours, and much time traveling away were taking on my family!

Lockport Mennonite Church.

That year I had an accident on the first of April—that special day called April Fool's Day! I shouldn't have survived. I had eight broken ribs! But God healed my injuries. Eight minister friends of mine came into my hospital room, anointed me with oil, and prayed healing prayers over me. The medical staff told me I'd be laid up for months, but I was only in there about a week. By God's miraculous healing power, the following Sunday I was in church preaching! Two weeks later, I was pitching for a key game.

Life was going well. I thought nothing could go wrong but everything did! At the end of the year, I lost the vote to be ordained by just a few votes. I was devastated! And nobody would talk about it, not even me! I didn't feel like a complete person without a ministry.

I became the administrator of a youth center for troubled youth, run by the courts for a number of years. Then we found a pastorate position for me at a tiny country church. I served there a couple years. But my heart was still back at Lockport. Then I got the opportunity to apply for a position in my hometown area. I was elated. I felt like I was coming full circle! But shockingly, I was suddenly dropped before they even brought me to a vote. They gave me no explanation. I was totally disheartened—so much so that I left the ministry. I ended up selling cars, bringing in good income, but it brought me no joy.

It wasn't long after my resignation that our marriage fell apart. I was getting frustrated to the point that I found myself yelling at my wife and kids. My emotions were controlling me, instead of me controlling my emotions. So now I had lost everything, my job, my ministry, and worst of all my family. After my divorce, I didn't go to church for a year.

I continued selling cars, doing so well that I made the best money in my life! But there was no joy in the Lord. I was not in God's eternal purposes or bottom line. I was in the worst spirit and attitude of my life. I hated life, God, and everyone. I especially hated myself. I couldn't forgive or let go. I felt like my life was over. God had given me a chance in life, but I had struck out! I had a lot of church people confirm what I believed: that you can't preach after you are divorced. Everything in life to me was about performance, and I could no longer perform!

The man who did so well in sports and wanted to do better yet in ministry was done! You could put a fork in me and see! I knew I would always feel second best. I knew that in baseball I had gone as far as the gift could take me, but in ministry I had barely begun to fulfill the potential of the gift. In other words, I had totally failed the gift God had given me. I believed I would now never get an "Atta boy!" from God or others or myself again. The

outgoing, smiling, joyful man was now living in isolation. I wanted to be left alone. I didn't have to worry because most church people did leave me alone.

"What's the bottom line?" was the question I was asked the most in my twelve years of sales! What was God's bottom line in my life? Why was Jesus, the Light of God, poking holes in my darkness? Why was the spirit and attitude of God different from mine and most other people's? How was God going to get me to perceive, understand, and apply His eternal purposes? And when?

Chrysler has him glowing

Art Zehr has moved back to the North Country from his old job at Mount Clemens Dodge—he's now selling Chrysler near Lapeer, and says it's easier selling to his neighbors.

God was training me in the minor leagues for Kingdom work. He was helping me to be "street smart." Chrysler, not the church had me "glowing." But actually, I wasn't glowing at all as you can see in the photo. There was a gnawing in my heart that kept speaking to me. I knew that my life was intended to be more—much more! And I was right. My life was intended to be more than I could ever dream or imagine. God

again offered me grace—the life I always wanted—one that redeems emptiness and overflows with hope. He offered me both love and forgiveness.

God was showing me what I was and what I was meant to be. Jesus is a window through which we see the very nature of God; and a mirror revealing our human possibility by picturing our fallenness and then the image of our divine destiny.

Metamorphosis means, "a dramatic change through struggle." God's method is of changing you from the inside out. God is after changing you and He isn't going to wait very much longer. God is in the change business. And if you do not submit, you will find out that God has a way of making you want to change. For when the pain of remaining the same is greater than the pain of changing, you will have a dramatic change. "Something takes place inside the cocoon. There is a dramatic struggle and that ugly worm one day becomes a beautiful butterfly."

Christianity is not a theory or a philosophy of life. Christianity is a living process. The minute you said, "yes" to Christ; the minute you said you "belong" to Him, it became a lifestyle. God calls us to be an organic church. What's organic? It's living and breathing.

I knew I was not living and breathing the abundant life. I had to change! I knew I couldn't change myself! I had tried that too many times. I needed help! Where could I turn? The following answers from an answering machine were supposedly used at the New York Psychiatric Hotline. It's hard hitting, but to the point.

Welcome to the Psychiatric Hotline!
If you are obsessive/compulsive, press 1 repeatedly.
If you are co-dependent, ask someone to press 1.
If you are multiple personalities, press 3,4,5, and 6.
If you are a paranoid/delusional, we know who you are and
    what you want. Stay on the line until we trace the call.
If you are a schizophrenic, listen carefully and a little voice
    will tell you which number to press.

If you are a manic-depressive, it doesn't matter which number you press, no one will answer anyway.

*O*ops! I found out that was not the right answer. Maybe I pushed the wrong button. Should I do it again? Was I too late? This reminds me of a story.

Oooops!

Source Unknown

A priest was being honored at his retirement dinner after 25 years in the parish. A leading local politician and member of the congregation was chosen to make the presentation and give a little speech at the dinner. He was delayed so the priest decided to say his own few words while they waited.

"I got my first impression of the parish from the first confession I heard here. I thought I had been assigned to a terrible place. The very first person who entered my confessional told me he had stolen a television set and, when stopped by the police, had almost murdered the officer. He had stolen money from his parents, embezzled from his place of business, and taken illegal drugs. I was appalled. But as the days went on I knew that my people were not all like that and I had, indeed, come to a fine parish full of good and loving people."

Just as the priest finished his talk, the politician arrived full of apologies at being late. He immediately began to make the presentation and give his talk. "I'll never forget the first day our parish priest arrived, " said the politician. "In fact, I had the honor of being the first one to go to him in confession."

If I wasn't too late, maybe I could try God's answer in Jesus. But, I had relapsed so many times! Would He give me another chance? "God, where do I go, what do I do? Can you ever use me again?"

Jesus Gives Second Chances

I battled guilt and shame, finding it difficult to forgive myself. I made the mistake of measuring Christ's forgiveness by the level of acceptance I felt from other believers. And because others kept their distance, I wandered in a wasteland of self-pity and rejection for many years.

The enemy nearly destroyed me with the lie that my sins were greater than Christ's work on the cross. Satan wanted me to believe I had forfeited my place within the Body of Christ and all hope for healing and reconciliation was lost.

But Jesus didn't give up on me. Just like He did for Zaccheus (Luke 19:1-10), the adulteress woman (John 8:1-11), and many others, Jesus offered me another chance. He spoke to my heart that my sins were forgiven and it was time for me to turn my attention to building the Kingdom of God and offering hope to others who had failed.

Those who make life-altering mistakes can anticipate a season of shame, sorrow, and separation. But as 2 Corinthians 2:5-11 says, our goal within the Body of Christ is repentance, reconciliation, and restoration! The power to overcome sin will never be found in a person's own determination or wisdom. Freedom from the bondage of sin only comes through surrender to God.

Our only hope of overcoming habitual sin is to replace our love for sin with a consuming love for God. Until this love seizes the soul, we will never experience a driving passion for holiness.

Only when we look into Christ's lovely face will we find a love that will eclipse our love of sin and self.

So, herein lies the answer. It is to see Jesus; to fall in love with "the Lover of my soul." *My eyes are fixed on you, Oh Sovereign Lord* (Psalm 141:8 NIV). This is the bottom line. Jesus is about grace.

A. Gram Ikin, in her book, *Victory Over Suffering,* states that "a Christian can respond to trouble in one of three ways: break down, break out, or break through. Breaking down means becoming ill and requiring care. Breaking out means resorting to hostile behavior toward others. Breaking through means acting with faith and hope in God's eventual purpose (2 Cor. 4:7-14)."

An off-the-wall experience opened the door to a new dimension of spiritual power and authority for me. God heard my cry. He knew how upset I was and He wanted me to know it was also breaking His Heart! When we intercede, He intervenes.

It was 1987. I was at the lowest point in my life. I had not preached for about eight years. Instead I had been the sales manager at the Chrysler, Dodge, Plymouth dealership in Lapeer, MI. I was doing great at my job, getting great honors and awards for the highest sales. I should have felt on top of the world. But I didn't. I felt empty inside. I had no happiness. I didn't like the thought of being stuck selling cars for the rest of my life.

My parents were coming to visit me. I knew Mom would notice my spirits were down. I knew the subject of me being a preacher would come up again and I dreaded it. My mom, a very Godly woman, told me after they arrived, "Art, you need to let go of the ministry idea. You're

doing well in car sales. Everything will be okay." She knew I was struggling emotionally. She knew I was caught in the desire to preach again. But she was going by tradition that said, because of my divorce, I could never be a minister again.

I said, "But, Mom. It's not okay. I don't have the joy of the Lord. I'm miserable."

That night I prayed, "Lord, please just take away the desire in me to preach because it is killing me. I give up. I just want to walk away and forget about ministry. Just take the desire away and I will accept the fact that I am to live a normal life and never preach again. I've got to know tonight. I've got to hear from You, God!!"

I went to bed feeling horribly down, wondering, "Is there a God who cares about me? Will He help me get out of the mess I'm in? Will He comfort me, forgive me, restore me, heal me?" I was at the end of my rope.

Who's voice are you listening to? It can't be Mom or Dad. It can't be the church. It can't be a denomination. We have to be careful who we listen to—even the best person. (My mom who has since passed away was a devoted, Godly woman. My dad still loves the Lord today.) If they're making the calls to the next pitch, it's not the right pitch. The voice we need to listen to is God's; deep speaking to deep; His Spirit imparting into our inner spirit.

I knew deep down that I was called by God. Because of that, no matter all the "Atta boys" I was getting from sales, they weren't helping me feel any better. I wondered, "Was it really true that *the gifts and the calling of God are irrevocable* (Rom. 11:29)— even in my messed up case?

From the vantage point of the years later, looking back, I can say that the road of life I had traveled was not a straight line. It had many a turn and twist and bump and detour. Christians do not arrive at maturity all at once. Our life is a walk!

In searching for God's purpose, I see that when I came to Jesus, stripped of pretensions, with a needy spirit, ready to listen to Him, and to receive what He had for me, He met me at my point of need. God doesn't visit us until we're real with Him, and He always starts with where we're at.

I am well aware that we don't get everything we ask for; we have to ask according to God's will. But let us not illogically dodge the fact that we often go without things God wants us to have right now today because we fail to ask. Too seldom do we get honest enough to admit, "Lord, I can't handle this alone." "Jesus, help me! I can't take it anymore!"

That evening when I was at my lowest point, confounded by obstacles, and bewildered by the darkness that surrounded me, I discovered an astonishing truth: God is attracted to weakness. He can't resist those who humbly and honestly admit how desperately they need Him. Our weakness, in fact, makes room for His power. In fact, God's first people were not called, "Jews" or "the Children of Israel" or "Hebrews." In the very beginning their original name was, "those who called on the name of the Lord." After Moses came down from Mount Sinai, calling on God became an earmark of his people's successes. The patriarch spotlighted this most dramatically in his farewell address: *What other nation is so great as to have their gods near them the way the LORD our God is near us whenever we pray to him?* (Deut. 4:7).

The other nations may have had better chariots and horses and better weaponry, but that wouldn't matter in the end. They didn't have what Israel had: a God who responded when they called upon Him. I needed to learn that God was not only concerned about whether or not I was doing His work, but also how and why I was doing it. Why was I pastoring and in what spirit? I was out of sync with the purposes of the Lord!

In my spirit of brokenness and calling on God, I freely expressed my need. I wanted to KNOW would God pick me back up and give me a second chance? I desired life, joy, a sense of family, and love. Could God still change people and deliver them from evil? A.W. Tozer says in his book, *Divine Conquest*, Living Books, 1995:

> "The desire to be filled must be all-consuming. … Only the hopeless will benefit. … For all who will hear, for all who will obey, here is God's answer to our need—HIMSELF.
>
> We cannot think rightly of God until we begin to think of Him as always being there, and there first.
>
> … Wherever faith has been original; wherever it has proved itself to be real, it has invariably had upon it a sense of the "present God" … [an] actual encounter with a real person.

My Real Encounter with the Real God

In my despair, God met me. I went to sleep praying and God intervened (Heb. 4:16). He gave me a dream. In the dream He gave me a baseball sermon. He told me who the players were, what their line-up was, and what their positions were. It was such a vivid, real dream. It was as if God were in the room speaking directly to me. This was a totally new experience to me because up to that point I didn't believe that God speaks to people today. I had even preached against people hearing God's voice. God told me in the dream that I would preach this sermon all over the world starting with three times that weekend.

When I woke up, I immediately wrote down the players' line-up and what God told me about them. Here is what I wrote.

DH	1. David	Heart
2b	2. Abel	Sacrifice
LF	3. Enoch	Please God
RF	4. Noah	Grace
C	5. Abraham	Obeyed
1b	6. Isaac	Promise
3b	7. Jacob	Builder and maker
S.S.	8. Joseph	Instructions for future
CF	9. Moses	Choosing

Imagine my shock the next day when I was looking in the Scripture and saw that the line-up God gave me in the dream was almost exactly the same as the line up in Hebrews 11!

I woke up and was just dazed. I was scared to death. You know it's not just a burning bush for Moses. God has a burning bush for all of us.

The original list on the original slip of paper. I have kept this folded up in my wallet ever since the dream because I didn't ever want to forget that night.

Do you think I told anybody about the dream? They had laughed at me before. I was afraid they would look at me and say "It's not God." I had no plans to tell anyone.

I went to work that day and I sat down at my desk which was in a large room with all the other sales desks. I sat there and wondered what God would do. One of the sales associates asked, "What's wrong with you today, Art?" He could've asked what's right about me because I was quiet.

I was no longer thinking my ideas. I was broken. And I was saying, "Okay, God. What's the next step? What pitch are

you going to throw?" I wondered how He was going to throw it and where He was going to throw it. I knew He was going to do something.

I heard the secretary's voice over the loudspeaker, "Phone call for Art Zehr." I expected it to be a customer.

"Hello?"

"Hello, Art, this is Richard Sullivan." I was shocked. Richard was a CPA and attorney. He was a very well-respected man in the Catholic circles in that community—actually one of the most respected mature Christians in the county. He was the president of Full Gospel Businessmen's chapter of Lapeer, MI. I had tremendous respect for this man. He's calling me?!!! That was shocking enough, but what he said next blew me away. "I want you to preach next Sunday afternoon at 2 pm at the prison."

He had been in prison ministry for years. This was a brand-new large men's facility right on the outskirts of Lapeer. He had just been given permission to hold services there with the privilege and responsibility to bring groups in to give talks, do Bible studies, programs, etc. This was to be their first such service in this new prison. "God told me you have a sermon. Do you have one?" I had to admit I did. I agreed to his request. I was a deer in the headlights! Completely stunned! I was realizing I had to rethink all my theology about God speaking to people today.

That was one time, but the dream said three times. I knew if this was of God, there would be two more experiences like that. I was scared.

The next day eating out with my parents, as we were going in, the man I was to encounter next was coming out. It was the United Methodist pastor, James Timmons. "Art, I just got done mentioning your name to Beth. The district director is looking for an emergency fill-in for two churches in the Port Huron area."

I was no longer a deer in the headlights, I was now being hit by the car! Even I can do one plus two and get three. A pastor's

26-year-old son had died. He normally preached at three small churches. So, I was thinking, *But the dream said three; this is four.* I was also wondering how I could do that preaching and get back to the prison in time.

Then he said, "They have arranged for two of the services to be combined, so we need you at 9 and 11 am."

"How far away is it? I've got to be back by 2 pm because I'm preaching at the prison."

He said, "You will be back by 12:30. God laid you on my mind. I know that you went through some pain. And I don't think God wastes pain." [He doesn't waste pain, folks. He turns all things around for good.]

That was the three times for the weekend!! I preached three times that Sunday, all in one day and I hadn't preached for eight years.

As I was getting ready for the services, I began to feel led on how God wanted me to fill out the dream more.

David—Heart—Designated Hitter
Abel—Spirit of Sacrifice—Second Base
Enoch—Walked with God—Left Field
Noah—Godly Fear—Right Field
Abraham—Obedience—Catcher
Isaac—Looking into the Future—First Base
Jacob—Blessed Others—Third Base
Joseph—Promises of God—Short Stop
Moses—Choices—Center Field

*H*ow God does things, when He does them, and in what manner are up to Him. The Name of Jesus, the Power of His Blood, and the prayer of faith have not lost their power over the centuries. God will do what only **He** can do! God was trying to get me back on track, so He urged me to "learn from us the meaning of the saying, 'Do not go beyond what is written'" (I Cor. 4:6). His visit to me had no other foundation than Scripture. He was calling

me to preach "the Good News about the Lord Jesus" and "the Lord's hand" was going to be with me (Acts 11:20-21).

Of course, God gave me no permission whatsoever to adjust the message of the Gospel. I must faithfully and boldly proclaim that sin is real, but Jesus forgives those who confess. When I preached I was not to finesse the people. My communication was not to be "cool" or "soothing." I was to "pitch" the words with God's anointing aimed for a piercing of the heart, for conviction of sin. God only called me to do His work proclaiming His Word to people He loves, under the anointing and power of the Holy Spirit to produce results that only He can bring about. Graciously and firmly, we have to speak the truth in love.

The message of the cross will always be foolishness to some and a stumbling block to others. No one is smarter than God. When He says to do His work in His way, we can be assured that He will produce His results for His glory. God knows exactly what we need to do and expects us to trust and obey Him in childlike simplicity.

I was to call upon God to revolutionize me in a supernatural way. I was to have a faith that is based not just on the cross, but also on the empty tomb. I had a lack of spiritual vitality and of fervency, and of closeness to the Lord. God wanted me to become like Him.

The Spirit of God is a Spirit of mercy, of compassion, and of reaching out. I was surprised by the power of a loving Almighty God. That evening I became filled with the Holy Spirit. God, the Holy Spirit does unusual things, and He does not always notify us in advance (Rom. 8:14).

I am glad I had the passion to call upon the Lord and I'm still in awe at how He opened the Heavens and showed Himself so powerfully. He showed me the Throne of Grace where He acts in people's lives (John 5:39, 40). I knew the written Word of God

very well, but not the Living Word. The Scriptures are not so much the goal as they are an arrow that points us to the life-changing Christ. The teaching of sound doctrine is a prelude, if you will, to the supernatural. It is also a guide, a set of boundaries to keep emotion and exuberance within proper channels (2 Cor. 3:6).

I was to get in the Diamond of Grace and play ball there. No more deadness or fanaticism. The old saying is true: "If you have only the Word, you dry up. If you have only the Spirit, you blow up. But if you have both, you grow up." I could no longer succumb to fear of the Holy Spirit. William Law bluntly declared more than 200 years ago that the church of his day was "in the same apostasy that characterized the Jewish nation .... The nation of Israel refused Him who was the substance and fulfilling of all that was taught in their Law and prophets. The Christian church is in a fallen state for the same rejection of the Holy Spirit." He said further that just as the Jewish leaders refused Jesus and quoted Scripture to prove their point, "so church leaders today reject the demonstration and power of the Holy Spirit in the name of sound doctrine" (William Law, *The Power of the Spirit,* reprint Fort Washington, PA, Christian Literature Crusade ,1971, p. 23).

I cried for more. I implored God to manifest Himself to me like He did to those Heroes of Faith.

And He did reveal more truth to me. After my spiritual awakening, He showed me that I needed to tear down the accumulated junk in my soul. My rationalizing had to cease. I had to start seeing my sinful debris—trash I had not noticed before. I had to deal with long-buried issues.

Now whenever I get hungry to truly know the Lord more, the Holy Spirit again quickly puts a shovel and broom into my hands. Whatever grieves God has to go. Whatever He approves of stays and has to be first in my life. People who have a seeking heart

still make mistakes. But their reaction to rebuke and correction shows the condition of that heart. Anything and everything is possible with God, if we approach Him with a broken spirit. We must humble ourselves, get rid of the debris in our lives, and keep leaning on Him instead of our own understanding.

People who do this are role models for us today. The Hebrew Hall of Faith heroes did not just sit back as many do today, saying, "He'll fulfill His Word." They stepped up and took action in obedience to the Lord. They understood that God's work in the world is usually a joint project (team effort). He works with us as we yield ourselves to work (play ball) with Him. These Hall of Faith heroes risked their lives. They left their families and headed for dangerous territory. The Bible uses a special word to describe what they did: "exploits" (2 Sam. 23:17,20, 22 NIV). I know I am a common person, but I desire ("set my heart") to do uncommon things for God.

God gave me a verse to close the sermon for that weekend: *"Come thou with us, and we will do thee good, for the Lord hath spoken good concerning Israel"* (Numbers 10:29 KJV). God wanted me to encourage those at the church who had just lost a dear one and those in the prison that He is walking with them; that when we choose to follow God and His people, He will do us good.

I wrote the verse on the back of the same slip of paper on which I had written the line-up from the dream. I wanted to make sure I remembered to close with that verse. When I gave the sermon, the only notes I had with me were on that little slip of paper.

Chapter 3

Commissioned

*W*hen I was young, I wanted to be a major league baseball pitcher. I thought that if I played ball and was careful to perform well and practice well, I could make the major leagues. But my curve ball usually curved more after it was hit than before. So, it became obvious that I would never make the big leagues.

Then God called me to the ministry. To me that was more important than sports. And I wanted to see what all I could "do" for God. I had been told and firmly believed that reading the Word of God was important. I read it six times in one year, and I preached in 26 different places in one year early in my ministry. I went all out zealously, but I made a mess for God because I did not understand grace. And because I didn't understand grace, God had to let me be broken, so He could more nobly rebuild me.

But now God was calling me to use my baseball experience as a premise for my sermon.

Diamond of Grace

The first thing I had to learn was about the diamond of grace. Up to that point, as I said earlier, I had been on a diamond of performance. I had a religious spirit. It was all about "Do do do!" I had been a performance-based pastor. Now, I'm not saying that you don't have to perform. If a baseball player doesn't perform, he gets sent back to the minors or is let go. But on God's diamond of grace, *being* always comes ahead of *doing*. I had to get back to God's grace. Nothing is more fundamental than the foundation of Grace.

Grace is the foundation. There are the rules of the game, but they are based on grace. There is a balance here that is hard for us to comprehend. The Law book couldn't save us, but it is perfect. It tutors us. God sent Jesus to us as a baby—small enough for us to relate, because God wants a relationship with us. Jesus died so we can have grace, and then He sent the Holy Spirit so we can now not only be in relationship, but we can also be empowered, and our minds can be opened to understand grace.

I've played on a lot of ball diamonds made of a lot of different materials. But God's is grace—a material never used before. He spoke grace. This is the most important thing God told me, and I didn't totally understand it then, and I probably still don't totally understand it, but I'm giving it here to the degree in which I do understand it. The soil of God's ball diamond is grace. It's the most important thing I'm saying today. Some of the diamonds I've played on were well groomed. Some weren't. Some were dangerous because they had rocks. You can get hurt playing on them. I have a few scars on my shins from ground balls hitting rocks and bouncing up to hit my legs. The Holy Spirit keeps helping us clean and groom our diamonds. (On my earliest ball diamond, I had trash cans right there for clearing away the clutter.)

I loved baseball so much I would play on any kind of dia-mond. even one with the trash cans near home-plate.

Some diamonds are not made of good materials. One scar I have is from a new, artificial infield diamond with an outfield that had not been properly raked—not professionally manicured. The ball hit the lip of the infield diamond that was sticking up, causing the ball to turn course and hit my right leg instead of my glove.

God's infield and outfield material is the best. His grace is everywhere. We can play ball anywhere. But we are all going to carry some scars while we are learning to choose grace.

What is Grace? First of all, it is Jesus' sacrifice on the cross that brought grace to us. This is grace, that Jesus' shed Blood doesn't just cover our sins, it washes them away. When we receive what He has done, we stand before Him as clean and white as if we never, ever did anything wrong our whole lives. *For by grace you have been saved through faith, and that not of yourselves; it is the gift of God, not of works, lest anyone should boast* (Eph. 2:8-9).

Then His grace keeps us from being condemned when we stumble and sin again. *There is therefore now no condemnation to those who are in Christ Jesus* (Rom. 8:1). *If we confess our sins, He is faithful and just to forgive us our sins and to cleanse us from all unrighteousness* (1 John 1:9).

Lastly, here is a new definition of grace that God gave me: Grace is God's help to us in whatever area we need help. We can't help ourselves. Others can't help us, so get your eyes off others and get your eyes off yourself. God's "grace is sufficient for us (2 Cor. 12:9). Grace is love; grace is compassion; grace is mercy and forgiveness. Jesus extends it to us. We need to extend it to others.

In God's grace, we don't have to hide our scars. Jesus showed His scars to His disciples.

....They [the disciples] were hiding for fear of the Jews. The religious system of their day had made them so afraid of their own faith. ... He is risen and

because He has risen, you can rise out of your situation. You can rise out of your defeat. You can rise out of your sin. ... Jesus goes to where the disciples are hiding. He does something remarkable. As evidence to them that He is, He shows them the scars. He says this is the evidence of My power. ...

I think that the story of Thomas tells us something critical. It tells us that we are in the midst of a generation that will never believe until they see the scars. They've seen our programs. They've heard our music. They've watched our dancing. They've heard our preaching. They see our faith. They know that we are happy most of the time. They know these things. But, they say that it is not enough for you to be happy, it's not enough for you to have good church, "I have got to see scars to believe." .... (From "Show Me Your Scars!" By Dr. Robert Costa, *Evangel Magazine*.)

In a ball diamond, there are chalk lines—the foul lines—coming on to the batter's box. I can get in the batter's box. The faith lines are there. It doesn't matter if you're left handed; it doesn't matter if you're right-handed, you can get on either side. God's diamond of grace is for "whosoever." How big is your ball diamond? God gives the faith and as we appropriate the faith, our diamond gets bigger.

What is faith? One of God's favorite words is the word "now." Hebrews 11:1 starts with that word. *Now, faith is the substance of things hoped for the evidence of things unseen.* Faith is accepting God's grace. And faith brings God pleasure. Our ball diamond will be as big as our faith. We have to meet God part of the way. We need to respond in our measure of faith. I've played in some diamonds where the fences are short. The minor league diamonds are short. Amazing feats are less likely to occur in smaller dimensions of faith.

The foul lines are there to help us not go too far. I used to think I needed to fight for God to help keep people inside the lines. But God doesn't even do that. We don't have to fight to keep people in line. We just need to do the part God gave us and not overreach. When you overreach, that's when you mess things up and you hurt people.

Our Four Bases

First Base
> Confession/Salvation/Being called/Believing:
> We are sinners. We cannot get started without coming through Jesus.
> Our perception is toward the outfield.

Second Base
> Repentance/Sanctification/Justification/Receiving the call: We are no longer babies; we are now children. We must turn from our sins. Some people have not turned. We must start learning from Jesus and the Holy Spirit and the Word.
> Our perception has changed. Our focus is now toward home plate.

Third Base
> Revelation/Perceiving God's judgement/ Maturing as a Christian / Experiencing God's Glory: The third-base coach is the Holy Spirit. A lot of people never get to third base. They are no longer looking to God for revelation.
> Third base is run totally different depending on the number of outs. Now our focus is on our Coach.

Home Plate
> Fruitfulness/Faithfulness/Bearing fruit: We are first a child, then a son, then a mature son. Mature Christians are those that overflow in fruitfulness. Reaching home plate is doing something that counts in the Kingdom. Our focus is on what we can do for God's Team.

We can get started with God when we confess that we are sinners. David realized he was a sinner in the eyes of God and needed to confess.

In baseball, once you get to second base, you have to look both ways to see which way to run. Second base is all about repentance. A lot of us in the Christian church never get that far. A person does not get to the scoring position—second base—until they repent and confess every known sin! We must have repentance working for us. And then to get as far as third, we must have the judgment of the Holy Spirit! Not our norm, but God's standards from God's Word! Not our judgment. Not the judgments of others, but God's judgments.

I had enough trouble with confession, and a horrible time with repentance. Did you have a difficult time turning around? I hadn't gotten to third base yet and I had been a preacher. I had preached in a lot of places about a lot of things. And I realized, "Man! In my life, according to the eyes of God, I'm not on third base yet."

You run third base totally different than all the other bases. When the ball is hit in the outfield, depending on how many outs there are, you don't run home. I've seen ball games lost because the runner on third base took off running before the ball was caught. This is where a lot of Christians don't get it, even mature Christians. They're going by their great ideas, but God has His plans. They say, "This is MY vision." We must die to our own visions before we can be resurrected. Most churches, most families, most individuals never get to third base. I didn't. That was a very humbling thing. It's why God allowed me to be broken.

God wants us to get to third base. We must be so sensitive to the Holy Spirit and to revelation. We must be ready to tag up. We must look at things differently than we did at the other bases because we do want to score, don't we? We do want to be productive for God, don't we? God wants us to score. We must be looking in the direction of the goal. Home plate is crucial. The whole purpose of getting on base is to score. Forget the glory of running the bases because it doesn't count until we step on that plate. It's not going to count. And we're not going to get there—until we're in tune to the Holy Spirit. It's from the fruit of—the by-product of—the Holy Spirit. It's not us. "It's not by power and might but by the Spirit." We can only be fruitful when the Holy Spirit bears fruit through us. To hit home plate—to be fruitful—comes by abiding in Christ; by the Holy Spirit getting us all the way so we can touch the plate and score. God doesn't just save souls, He saves lives. He saves every part of us. God desires His Spirit to touch and connect to our human spirit, so we can have oneness. God wants to finish what He has started!

*G*od is our owner and our pitcher. He is the builder and Creator. He's the architect. He's the one who gives out the calls. In our game analogy today, we can't let God bat because God never makes an out. It wouldn't be fair. Our team today, let's say, is with the American League. In the American League, they have ruled that a team can have a DH (designated hitter) hit for their pitcher. This is still not settled in the National League. Just recently (in Mar. 2012), a pitcher now in the National League, in a drill in spring training, broke a bone in his eye after bunting. He had not learned how to bunt correctly.

God, the owner and manager, is also the head coach. He picks the batting line-up. If you bat out of turn you're out. Each one in the line-up in Hebrews had to realize that they were not bigger or better than God, or that they knew more than God.

*S*o God is our owner, manager, and pitcher, but who are our base coaches? We need to know this before we play ball. Our

coaches are Jesus and the Holy Spirit. I've seen a lot of people play ball and they don't pay attention to the coaches. They just run around on their own. That doesn't work.

The Lord says, "Art , if you make a mistake, you listen to Me. I'm the coach. You forget about everything else. You get direction from Me! If you fall down, just get back up. Do you ever fall down and turn back? No. Get back up and listen to your coaches as to which way to run."

I said that God does not bat, but God can pitch to whomever He wants. So God picks who He wants to bat first, to be His designated hitter, and He picks David. In Hebrews 11:32 you see his name so you know he is on the team. But in today's line up, he's batting leadoff.

Our first-base coach is none other than Jesus Christ the perfecter of our faith; the One that helped David to confess; the One that David looked forward to in grace. David knew his life needed to be rebuilt. So David confessed and repented and he had a different judgment of himself and he scored. And God picks him as our leading player—to lead off.

Now when you pick a ball team, you're very careful of your selection of the first player. He's the catalyst of the team. That lead-off guy sets the tone. You want to get him on base. And David was a hit with God. He was the apple of God's eye. So he starts off today's game batting for God with a hit.

Now why did God pick David? Because he was the best? No. David was the catalyst that God is picking. David wasn't perfect. He did things that are probably worse than any sinful acts you've done. But God has called him. If David can make it, so can we.

David finally gets to a place in his life where he made sure he always had everything cleared between him and God. It was the most important thing to him. This is why God picks him as the catalyst—he confessed. He is a DH. He is not playing the field. He is just batting first.

Why is David a hit with God—the apple of God's eye? Because of his heart. It's all about the heart! See, God looks at our heart. The main thing that God wants in all of us is our heart. The whole thing that matters in our families, in our churches, is our heart. We don't get to see God until our heart is right. On this team, God was so pleased with David's heart—a heart that worshipped Him. David committed a lot of sin, but every time he fell down and got back up, he became a better ball player. He became the great catalyst. And today he starts off our game. He's a hit with God because his heart is right.

Is your heart right like David's was? Have you been reborn in your spirit? David had to confess, repent, judge, have faithfulness with God, and be totally transformed and rebuilt by the Spirit of God. Have you been born by the Holy Spirit? If you've not, I'm praying the Holy Spirit will come upon you and you will come to God's altar to be reborn today.

We must be broken. Are we? Here's a test to see.

1. Am I willing to let go of my dreams and ambitions if such is God's will? _____
2. Am I defensive when accused, criticized, or misunderstood? _____
3. Am I coveting what others have instead of waiting for heaven's rewards? _____
4. Am I forgiving when offended, with or without an apology? _____
5. Am I thinking of others first out of love? _____
6. Am I proudly appearing as though I am always right or know all the answers? _____
7. Am I being silent regarding self-promotion and letting God do my public relations? _____

8. Am I daily saying, "God, whatever it takes, I'm willing to submit to your leadership?" _____

9. Am I expressing joy in the difficulties that serve to refine me? _____

10. Am I taking risks out of obedience to Christ instead of giving in to fear, pride, or denial? _____

11. What challenges do you face when trying to trust God rather than yourself? How has adopting a humble attitude helped you trust God more?

In what ways has God been "breaking" you lately, and how do you see that the experience is reshaping who you are? _____

_____

_____

_____

_____

_____

_____

_____

_____

Test by WAI "Exploring Worship" 6/17/04.

The next batter, you can see in the next verse, is Abel. What does Abel do in the line-up today? He sacrifices. Now most teams put a good bunter as their number two hitter. In fact, most second batters are the best bunters on the team. They bunt to make sure the first base runner gets to second. Often he will not make it to base himself, getting tagged out. They sacrifice.

Now we make a mistake a lot of times as church people by thinking that everybody is called to do exploits for God. We all can! Actually, it is God who does exploits through us. He does do them through certain players. But not everybody bats fourth. Abel bats second. And the reason why Abel is so successful, listen to this. Listen to Abel's attitude and spirit because some of you are Abels. You're trying to be the clean-up hitter, but God has called you to bat second. God called Abel to sacrifice.

The writer of Hebrews gives Abel as our first example. He had a spirit of sacrifice. And his sacrifice was more acceptable to God than others. Now, I've managed many years and I've given the flash line many times for someone to sacrifice. But they don't want to. "I want to hit the ball. I want to hit a home run!" "I want my portion! I've got my idea!! I'm not going to sacrifice." They weren't willing to sacrifice. His was an acceptable sacrifice. He considered how he could sacrifice. When we sacrifice what God asks of us, He will often resurrect it. If it's of God, there will be unity in the whole church on it. If there's a split, we all lose. We all have to do our part.

So Abel sacrificed. Did you ever see people who sacrifice? I mean when's the last time you celebrated someone's offering of sacrifice or when you had to sacrifice?

Abel considered where he should bunt. He considered whether it was better to bunt toward first or third or where. He asked himself, what will help the team the most? He cared about God's team. He cared about what God was doing. He made an out, but the team of God went ahead. It's not about you! It's about the team! You've got to be part of the team.

If we really want to make the team, isn't it God's call to what position we play and where we bat? Shouldn't it be God's decision? And God did decide on Abel, that His call was for Abel to give a living sacrifice.

Now Abel was not picked because he was the older brother. It had nothing to do with that. It had everything to do with his spirit and his heart. And the Word of God says this, "His gift lives on." Six millenniums later we read that his gift lives on. Do you want to do something for God that will live on? The spirit of sacrifice

67

never changes. Customs change. Manners change. Parents change. Sacrifices never change.

Batting second is Abel, our second basemen. He gave with a spirit of sacrifice. He made the first out in today's ball game. He made the first out and yet it lived on forever. He helped the team. Some of us are making outs and we're crying about it. Quit crying. Did it advance the Kingdom of God? Did it advance the team for God's glory? Then be willing to make an out for the team! And quit worrying about the home run! I learned that the hard way. Cain just gave acknowledgement. He just gave a gift. But Abel gave an acceptable gift. God counted him as righteous and his gift lives on. Are you willing to give sacrifices?

How much do you encourage your ball players and teammates when they make an out? Do you want to encourage them so they will want to bat again?

Will this change your whole attitude on sacrifices? I hope it will help you to quit judging others for their sacrifices and making outs. This batter made an out and it lives on. He helped the team. Too many times we're judgmental on those who make outs and yet they help God's team. Abel chose to give a living, acceptable, worship sacrifice out of his heart.

I hear the biggest argument in churches today is that people don't know how to worship. Who are we to judge? God's Spirit and grace is the only thing that will help us to worship. Others may worship differently than we do. There are many ways to worship God, as long as it comes out of the heart. Out of his spirit and heart, Abel worshipped God. And his gift carries on.

If you want to get on God's Hall of Fame list, you need to obey God's batting order even if it means you have to bat second. What in your life is going to last after you are gone? What are you living for that will never die?

Batting third, I'm wondering who. Teams pick their best hitter for third. The pure hitter with the highest average that can do the best thing for the team, they put them in that number three spot. And the writer of Hebrews makes no exception. He picks the most pure person with the highest average, Enoch. Enoch is batting third today for us.

Enoch walked in such faith that it pleased God. It pleased God!! And God let him know it. God let him know that He was very pleased with his walk. A lot of us will start off with God. But faith is also a walk. It's a continuation. It's a choice in the graces of God. Grace is the ability of God, the power of God, the strength of God for us to continue on. Enoch chose to continue on. Enoch had such a fellowship, such a purity, such harmony that he walked with God. He was in God's presence every where he would go. He would sense God's presence. How well are you aware of God's presence in every situation? No matter how bad, no matter what, His presence is there. Was it not in the belly of the whale with Jonah?

A professional hitter never wastes an AB (at bat). He tries to do the most for his team when he is at bat. Enoch never gave away an AB. He did the best he could at every AB. He stayed focused and gave his best. He was in rhythm with God and with the team. Then he was translated! He was so much in love with God and God was so in love with him that God took him.

No wonder he is a Hall of Faith hitter. No wonder he could walk. And what did he do in today's game? He got a walk.

So, David got a hit. Abel sacrificed him to second. Enoch walked. We've got a guy on first and second, don't we? Let me show you some more about Enoch, because some of you are worrying about that. God checks things out several times before He makes a verdict. God is calling all of us to go to heaven. And relax. Scripture has told us that there has already been two tried

and tested ahead of time who have not died. Enoch was the first. He went on to heaven. He never died. There's been another. So we know the system of God works. Someday we too, in our spirits will be called home. God has checked it out. It works. It says there in Scripture that Enoch's body was not found. He went with God. He left. So our number three hitter is playing left field. He left. God, by the way, is looking for another left fielder. I don't know who He's going to call but He will call somebody.

*N*umber four! Who's going to bat after Enoch? In my managing experience, I've found that a lot of players would like to bat fourth. Every team looks for who they're going to put in that slot because that's their RBI man. That's their most productive guy. He gets the rest of them home. Now, we all want everybody to be somebody else—to play some other position. Sometimes it is because we want to play in their position. Or we think someone else would fit it better. But, we don't call ourselves to our positions. God calls each and every one of you to the position He has designed us for (Eph. 2:10). God knew who to call where. I want to be in the place that God wants me in the line-up. It's His call.

God picks a significant person to bat fourth. It's Noah. He's the next one listed. Why did God pick Noah to bat fourth? He needed a clean-up hitter and nothing cleans up more than grace. By the way, he's our right fielder. Because the Word of God says, God found him righteous. For "Noah was found right in the eyes of God." He cleaned up the situation. What cleans up like nothing else? Grace!

All of our lives, we as churches and as individuals and families need things cleaned up. We need to be right again with God—again with ourselves—and again with others. There's only one thing that will enable us to get right with God, ourselves, and others. It is grace. Nothing keeps us right except grace. We want everyone else to change in certain ways. And they want us to change. But the key is grace.

Noah had an assignment as a clean-up hitter. He was called by God to build an ark. It had never rained. Now I'm not against common sense. I'm not against intellect. I'm not against theories. But God showed me that day that theories don't always work. God showed me that day that there are times when He does things that are above common sense. There are times He does things above the mind. He said to me, "I called Noah to build an ark. Others laughed at him. And you're worrying about how they're laughing at you, Art? Can you imagine how they laughed at Noah?"

Noah built an ark. It took him over a hundred years. Yet he built it for the saving of himself and his family because he believed in the grace of God. And God called him to do something in a place that made no common sense.

Now, is that an excuse to use no common sense? Too many times we Christian people say, "Well, I've got to be above common sense." But you had better make sure if you're not using common sense that it's God's call, not yours, because if it is your own idea, you will fail. Noah had to know that it was God's call. The key to all this is God's call; God's call in faith and in His grace. Those are the fundamental principles. Let's not forget them.

Noah cleaned up the situation. I don't know what he got for a hit that time, but I know one thing, he got eight "ribbies" in this game on God's team. What is a "ribbie"? It's baseball talk for an RBI, a run batted in. There were eight who were saved. There were eight who scored successfully at home plate. So there were eight RBIs in that game.

Now something interesting about the life of Noah that we need to know is that he was divinely warned by God. Some people say, "Well, why did God do this?" Usually before God does something, He divinely warns. Before He punished the world, He warned people. Noah was one who responded in faith.

71

He did things different from anyone else in the world—everyone else around him. He did not follow them. He could've said, "This is ridiculous. It doesn't make any sense." Would you build a boat if it had never rained?

Again, I am not suggesting that we are not to follow common sense. Some people say, "Well, it must be of God because it doesn't make sense." Let me say it again. If it doesn't make sense, please do not do it unless you know it is God! Sometimes when it *does* make common sense, it could be of God!

Noah spent over a hundred years building an ark! Over a hundred years! Can you imagine people laughing at you for over a hundred years?

So Noah is our clean-up hitter, batting fourth and playing right field. I think he earns the spot, don't you? He built that boat, got all those animals in it, but there were only eight saved. I'm thankful He didn't come to me with that call. I'm not sure I want to bat clean-up. But I do want to be on the team.

Do you want to know what God's call is for you? I'm convinced that God has called each and every one of us to a position on the team that He will give us the ability to fulfill. God will find a field position for us to play and a spot for us in the batting order, if we respond in faith. Faith is the substance that pleases God. These people honored their faith and their faith honored them because they honored and pleased God. Isn't that exciting? That's what pleases God—our faith.

Noah

In the year 2005, the Lord came unto Noah, who was now living in the United States, and said, "Once again, the earth has become wicked and overpopulated, and I see the end of all flesh before me.

Build another Ark and save two of every living thing along with a few good humans."

He gave Noah the blueprints, saying, "You have six months to build the Ark before I will start the unending rain for 40 days and 40 nights."

Six months later, the Lord looked down and saw Noah weeping in his yard—but no Ark.

"Noah!" He roared, "I'm about to start the rain! Where is the Ark?"

"Forgive me, Lord," begged Noah, "but things have changed. I needed a building permit. I've been arguing with the inspector about the need for a sprinkler system. My neighbors claim that I've violated the neighborhood zoning laws by building the Ark in my yard and exceeding the height limitations. We had to go to the Development Appeal Board for a decision.

"Then the Department of Transportation demanded a bond be posted for the future costs of moving power lines and other overhead obstructions, to clear the passage for the Ark's move to the sea. I told them that the sea would be coming to us, but they would hear nothing of it.

"Getting the wood was another problem. There's a ban on cutting local trees in order to save the spotted owl. I tried to convince the environmentalists that I needed the wood to save the owls—but no go!

"When I started gathering animals, an animal rights group sued me. They insisted that I was confining wild animals against their will. They argued the accommodation was too restrictive, and it was cruel and inhumane to put so many animals in a confined space.

"Then the EPA ruled that I couldn't build the Ark until they'd conducted an environmental impact study on your proposed flood.

"I'm still trying to resolve a complaint with the

Human Rights Commission on how many minorities I'm supposed to hire for my building crew.

"Immigration and naturalization is checking the green-card status of most of the people who want to work.

"The trades unions say I can't use my sons. They insist I have to hire only Union workers with Ark-building experience.

"To make matters worse, the IRS seized all my assets, claiming I'm trying to leave the country illegally with endangered species.

"So, forgive me, Lord, but it would take at least ten years for me to finish this Ark."

Suddenly the skies cleared, the sun began to shine, and a rainbow stretched across the sky. Noah looked up in wonder and asked, "You mean you're not going to destroy the world?"

"No," said the Lord. "The government beat me to it."

Taken from a Mennonite Church bulletin, 2007.

*W*ho bats fifth? Who caught the seed of promise? Abraham did. When he caught it he became the foundational father of our faith. Now, every mother who loves their kid really does not want their kid to be a catcher. Why? It's a dangerous spot. They get hurt. They have to block pitches. A lot of bad things can happen.

A lot of bad things happened to Abraham. He was called out of idolatry. He was called to leave his family and his friends and everything. He went not knowing where he was going. Whenever you think you know and that you have arrived, you strike out. You must be open to change. Abraham had to make major changes and sacrifices.

As a catcher, you're squatting all the time. And Abraham didn't get some of his squats quite right. He didn't block all the pitches. When he went into Egypt the first time, he told someone that his wife was his sister. He's our foundation pilgrim father. Do you think he started off well? There's hope for us. He was called by God, yet he didn't just stop there. He went on to make many other errors. He passed a lot of balls.

It's hard catching God's pitches. It's hard enough catching the pitches of others and ourselves. I have a hard time catching others—to understand what they're saying. But to catch God? No one can hit God's pitches! But Abraham learned to catch God. It took him awhile. He didn't do it perfectly. In fact, he never learned to do it perfectly. But God had faith in this man of idolatry. He had faith in this man to make him the Hebrew father. We talk about the Mayflower and the Pilgrim people, but here's the Hebrew father of all fathers, Abraham, who caught the seed of promise; who learned how to catch God's pitches. He took God's call, not his own call, not someone else's call—God's call. And from that, God built a Hebrew people.

When He called Abraham, God didn't tell him the destination. *And he went out, not knowing where he was going* (Heb. 11:8).

Does that sound somewhat impractical in the atmosphere of present-day business life? Yet, according to Carlyle, he goes farthest who does not know where he is going; like John Wesley, for instance, who never dreamed when he went out that his quest would take him across the threshold of the Church of his fathers; or Martin Luther, who never conceived when he started that he was going out of the Roman Catholic into the Bible Free State; or the Pilgrims of the "Mayflower," who never thought as they embarked that they were to lay the foundations of the greatest Republic the world has ever seen.

Abraham did not know what would meet him on his life-long journey: the day of peril in Egypt when he would break down and disgrace himself; the day of dissension with Lot when he would prove his fidelity; the days of conflict with the Rephaim and the Zuzim and the Emim and the Horites, when he would overthrow them; the day of temptation when the king of Sodom would offer to make him rich; the day of sharpest sorrow when he would be called to show his supreme devotion by resigning his beloved son into the hands of the Lord—all these days were hidden from him as he entered upon the long journey. All that God required of him was that he would meet them as they came; not beforehand, in imagination, in promise and definite resolution, but at the appointed hour, in the crisis of trial then, and not till then, Abraham must face his conflict, and make his sacrifice, and hold fast his faith.

Not otherwise does God deal with us. He does not show us exactly what it will cost to obey Him. He asks us only to give what He calls for from day to day. Here is one sacrifice right in front of us that we must make now in order to serve God—some evil habit to be given up, some lust of the flesh to be crucified and slain; and that is our trial for today. But tomorrow that trial may be changed from a hardship into a blessing, it may become a joy and triumph to us; and another trial, new, different, unforeseen, may meet us in the way. Now, perhaps, it is poverty that you have to endure, fighting with its temptations to envy and discontent, and general rebellion against the order of the world; ten years hence, it may be wealth that will test you with its temptations to pride, and luxury, and self-reliance, and general arrogance toward your fellow-men. Now, it may be some selfish indulgence that you have to resign; tomorrow, it may be someone whom you love, from whom you must consent to part at the call of God. Today, it may be your ease, your comfort, your indolence that you must sacrifice for the sake of doing good in the world; tomorrow, it may be your activity, your energy, the work you delight in, that you must give up while sickness lays its heavy hand upon you, and bids you "stand and wait." Today one thing, tomorrow another thing; and God does not tell you what it will be: He calls you to go out into your adventure not knowing whither you go.

The Speaker's Bible, edited by Rev. Edward Hastings, M.A. and James Hastings, D.D., Baker Book House, Grand Rapids, Michigan, ISBN 0-8010-4036-1, Vol. 17 "Epistle to the Hebrews," pp. 232-234.

As catcher, Abraham is the only one that's looking out. All the rest are looking in. He looks at the field differently. He thinks differently from the rest. This is one of the things that make him a key player on this team. You often hear, "Awe, he's just a catcher on the team!" But the catcher is very vital. He has to be in tune to the pitcher and adjust to what pitches he calls. Abraham let God call the pitches. And whatever God called, Abraham tried to catch. God knows what pitch to throw. Will you catch the pitch that He wants to throw? Abraham learned how. And he became the foundational father!

God took a long time to give Abraham the promise. We usually think we've got to do things right now. Then finally along came Isaac! He's the promise! Okay God, I have the son You promised. Then God comes along and *really* challenges him, asking him to sacrifice what is dearest and most precious to him. But Abraham met the challenge with much faith. He became a tremendous catcher. There's more written about him than any other one in the heroes of faith. He became that good of a catcher.

Of course a study of Abraham could be a whole sermon of its own. But we've got to continue on with the game. We have two other foundational corners. We still need a first baseman. And Isaac plays first base. Isaac bats sixth.

Isaac was a strong, steady man. He trusted God quietly and steadily after a bumpy start. Some of us are called to just be strong and faithful at home.

Isaac didn't start out with a lot of faith. At first he had trouble trusting God to protect him and his wife, so he lied that she was his sister, just as his father had done. But he eventually learned how to let faith be an exercise—a gift from God—an active gift, not something we work up. It's not something we will. A lot of church people have the wrong definition of faith. They get pride in their faith. Isaac got pride in his faith thinking he could handle things his own way—by hiding the truth. It set him back.

But then he began to exercise faith in God alone and God began to bless him for it. God gave him a hundred-fold harvest in the midst of a famine (Gen. 26:1,12). He soon became a wealthy man—so much so that his neighbors began to be jealous and mistreat him. He lived in a desert land where water is a precious commodity. Yet his neighbors hated him so much that they cut off his water supply. Whenever he dug a new well, they either stopped it up or claimed it for themselves and wouldn't let him use it.

But each time, Isaac responded calmly. He didn't let their actions stir up anger or worry or unrest in his soul. Instead, secure in his faith, he just quietly dug a new well. God rewarded him by appearing to him and speaking to him, just as He had spoken to his father Abraham.

Isaac's unwavering faith, in the end, caused his enemies to give him honor and respect. They told him they could clearly see that God was with him (Gen. 26:28)! God is calling some to His team just to live a solid, steady life of faith to build up the faith of others. Your faithfulness, in the background though it may seem, might even lead destructive people to give glory to the Lord.

Isaac's problems weren't over when the water disputes were

settled. He had problems with his sons and was deceived by his wife's conniving. But God used all that to cause him in the end of his life when his faculties were failing to give the proper prophetic blessings to the proper sons. As Hebrews 11:20 (NRSV) says, *By faith Isaac invoked blessings for the future.*

Faith is a gift from God. It's God's Spirit and grace that will make our faith mature. Isaac learned how. He became a cornerstone, a foundational first baseman.

We can never reach our full destiny apart from the people or things or circumstances God puts in our lives. Without his trials, Isaac could not have been seen as a man of faith.

Jesus never hid the danger factor from His disciples. He told them that at the end of My road is a cross. If you're going to follow Me you're going to have to take up your cross. In the garden, Jesus wrestled with the danger of the crucifixion, but He does not back down. He says that the only way to win this battle is to confront evil on its own territory and beat the devil at his own game. He prays through the fear and the danger and submits Himself to the eternal will and purpose of Almighty God. As a result they put stripes on His back. They put a crown of thorns on His head. They beat Him. They spit on Him. The Bible tells us that they made Him carry the very cross that they would ultimately nail Him to. To make sure that He had suffered and died, they took a spear and stuck it in His side. Now I don't know what you think of that, but Jesus knew that He was going to Calvary. Jesus knew that He was going to suffer and die. Nevertheless, Jesus said because you couldn't come to me, I'm going to have to come to you through the danger, through the pain, through the risk and through the crucifixion.

Taken from "Show Me Your Scars!" By Dr. Robert Costa, in the newsletter of Evangel Christian Churches, Roseville, MI.

The Lord wants us to display faith in Him like a small child does in his father—faith in what Jesus has done for us and in what He will do for us. Here's an interesting story about childlike faith.

Kitten
(Source unknown)

A church pastor had a kitten that climbed up a tree and then was afraid to come down. He coaxed and offered warm milk, but the kitten would not come down. The tree was not sturdy enough to climb, so the pastor decided to tie a rope to the tree and then to his car and slowly drive away so the tree would bend down and he could reach up and get the kitten.

However, as the pastor moved the car forward, the rope broke, the tree went "boing" and the kitten sailed through the air out of sight. The pastor felt terrible. He walked all over the neighborhood asking people if they'd seen a little kitten. Nobody had. So he prayed, "Lord, I just commit this kitten to Your keeping," and went on with his business.

A few days later he met one of his church members at the grocery store. He was amazed to see cat food in her cart. Everyone knew she was a cat hater, so he asked her, "Why are you buying cat food if you hate cats so much?" She replied, "Pastor, you won't believe this, "and then she told him how her little girl had been begging her for a cat, but she kept refusing. Finally she told her little girl, "Well, if God gives you a cat, I'll let you keep it." She told the pastor, "I watched my child go out in the yard, get on her knees, and ask God for a cat. And really, pastor, you won't believe this, but I saw it with my own eyes. A kitten suddenly came flying out of the blue sky, with its paws outspread, and landed right in front of her." Never underestimate God's power or unique sense of humor!

God put this kitten in this girl's life! Maybe the girl's name was Starla! My daughter Starla prayed for kittens too. God's grace and promises come when we have faith to expect them. Ask a child, "Can you believe that God promised to give you something through me? If so, hold out your hand." Children have no problem believing. They immediately hold out their hands. We adults are much more skeptical.

*I*saac had twin sons. And again, God doesn't always pick the first or the best or the strongest or the one that others would pick. He picked a scoundrel—Jacob, our third baseman. Oh, wow! This guy had more errors—more deceit. He didn't trust in what God had said. He forgot that it was God's assignment that he being the second born would take over. He tried to help God and when we try to help God, we get in the way.

He took part in deceit to try to assist God. Then deceit came his way. Of course, when you play third base, you have a lot of deceiving hops. And he did—from his father-in-law, from himself, from women. Women! For fourteen years, he had struggles that had to do with women. He had a lot of bad hops in his life. (Hops are when a ground ball bounces. A bad hop is when it bounces in an unpredictable direction and hits you instead of your mit. This can cause serious injury.) "It's all their fault." A lot of women say that of men. Amen. We can blame all the hops on others in life.

Jacob had a horrible time getting past his errors and bad hops. He was in the minor league a long, long time. But finally, in the grace of God and the faith in God, Jacob got called up to

the major leagues. Most people didn't think he'd ever make it. But he finally got it. He finally went to the place of God's promises, of God's sure things in Christ.

> Here's a joke from a soloist who sang "Take Me Out To The Ballgame" for me in the seventh inning of this baseball sermon one of the times I preached it. She said, "Here's a really goofy joke I learned as a kid: 'What does a center fielder and a frog have in common? They both catch flies.' "

We're in the last half of the seventh inning and will soon be done. Jacob had a lot of problems. Abraham, Isaac, and Jacob, even though they were called by God, did not see the promises of God right away, yet they knew they would see them. They knew that God's promises were sure. Even though they lived in tents, they knew that God's promises would come to pass. The fulfillment of God's call does not always happen immediately. We have to choose to believe that God will deliver, if it is of Him. They continued to choose to go on.

It is beautiful when family and children can worship together. We have Abraham as the catcher and Isaac as the first baseman and Jacob as the third baseman. Well, I wonder who plays shortstop. It's Joseph.

We could say of Joseph that he was not a good hitter. In fact, he didn't hit it off well with his brothers at all. He was a horrible hitter with them! That's why he's batting eighth. But he was a tremendous fielder. He did a tremendous job fielding the promises of God.

The short stop is the only one on the team who is a connecting link between the infield and the outfield. God pointed that out to me. Wow!! That's exciting. But it's hard connecting the infield and the outfield. The short stop player is run into by more people than anyone else. "I understand that, God." That's why I know I'm a short stop. I run into people. When you are the short stop, people bump into you. When you are going out to get a fly ball, you keep going and keep going until someone calls you off or the catch is missed or someone catches it for you. Or you run towards the fly and smack! Two of you run into each other. We have to learn how to communicate in the church. "I got it. It's my ball."

We also have to learn not to argue, "No, it's your ball." You have to let go of your rights. And they have to know your rights. You have to play your spot, not someone else's spot. "But I do seven jobs in the church, or three, or five." No, you're called for one. That doesn't mean you can't do others. Sometimes we have to play other spots while someone else plays ours. Sometimes we need to learn how to play all the spots, but which spot does God want you to play in the church today? Or this year? You might be saying, "No, for life!" You like your position and you want to keep doing it. But God says, "No, it's not for life. It's one game at a time! It's one day at a time."

We've got to call those fly balls. "Well, I don't want to get hurt," you might say. Or your attitude might be, "You know, I've got to run and run until somebody calls me off." If that's your spot, okay. But you have to know where your place ends.

Joseph ran and ran. He ran ahead of his dreams and visions. And not many liked him. Many of us, like him, have a lot of problems and times of separation from family. Let's give it to God and let Him sort it out. God had a purpose for that time for Joseph. God sent him out ahead to save his whole family.

Joseph was the one who connected and saved the family. For God picked him and called him. And his call was different than all the rest. He was called to go into bondage. Oh, God had given him dreams and God had given him visions. Joseph didn't understand them all. People betrayed him and abandoned him, they did all kinds of things to him. But he's the one God called

and equipped for infield and outfield. He had range that included a jail, included being thrown into a well. But he was faithful to his position. He was a tremendous defensive player—not much of a hitter, but a great short stop. Oh what a job he did in fielding the promises of God. He did whatever it took. Others meant it for harm, but he believed God meant it for good. God turned it around. He was a connecting link. And the whole family got blessed because of his faith.

*A*s we can see here in Joseph's life, any trial a believer faces can ultimately bring glory to God because God can bring good out of any bad situation (Genesis 50:20). When trouble comes do you grumble and complain, and blame God? Or do you see your problems as opportunities to honor Him?

*L*et's go back to the diamond. I just want you to visualize for a second. Visualize those players now in those spots. Joseph is that short stop, right up there between repentance and revelation. He's the one that goes into the outfield. He's the one that went out ahead into Egypt. He had many calls. In fact, all in this Hall of Faith had many calls. But they paid attention to God's call, not the other calls.

What is the call of God for us? I had to come to the place and say, "God, what do You want me to do with the rest of my life? I tried it my way and it's not working." And there have been times since when I think, "Oh, I've got it now. I've got it all figured out. You don't have to worry. I know what I'm doing. Get out of my way. I know where I'm going." And then I get into trouble and fall flat on my back. That's when you fall down on the baseline out there, when you say, "I know what I'm doing." God replies, "No, you don't. Get on the base!"

Now before we go back to the other line-up, let me tell you some more about Joseph. You know, too many times you hear,

"Well, the guy can't hit worth a lick! What good is he on the church team?" Hey, Joseph was on the team because God sent him out ahead to save the whole family.

The one that you may wonder, "What is he doing on the team?" He may be the encourager. He may be there to help someone else. He doesn't give great bats. "Well, he can't help. He never gets a hit." I want to tell you one thing. It's a proven fact. You do not get to the World Series unless you've got a good short stop. It's a proven fact. I don't care whether they hit or not. They're not all hitters. Some good defensive short stops have gotten some teams to the World Series. You know this if you know baseball. So let's start looking at each other on the church team a little differently. How can we encourage each other? How can we be more understanding? That will help the team more than anything.

I know I'm putting this in baseball language and it's not for everyone. And that's okay. It's for me. It got my attention and helped me understand. And I'm hoping today that it will help you understand some of this.

*A*re we willing to allow God to change our thinking, feelings, and behavior, so our dreams may develop? God would like our part!

By the grace of God are we willing to choose the right pain, so that we may have healing and joy and harmonious love to God, ourselves and others?

Joseph's dreams needed the test of time and maturity. They needed refining, honing, and polishing. God did not tamper with the dream, but He did temper the dreamer. He did not remove the dreams, but He did refine both the dream and the dreamer. Just as God was in the dream, so God was in the refining process.

Will you be open to the refining process?

God engineers our circumstances. Joseph had a dream. The dream got badly damaged at Dothan. What pulled Joseph through the next thirteen years of struggle and suffering? God's yes and his dream. Joseph had a dream and he would have never made it without one. And neither will any of us.

Seducers of the Dream!
- Self pity
- Anger, Unforgiveness and Bitterness
- Fear and worry
- Yielding to temptation. "Oh if I'd only known that someday I would meet a wonderful guy or gal like _____!"

Factors that held Joseph steady!
- Goal of sexual purity
- Sense of loyalty and responsibility and not wanting to sin against God

Repairing Broken Dreams
- Receive God's full and free forgiveness.
- Keep the darkness out of our hearts!
- We can't control what happens, but we can choose the right response to it.

How should we respond to what is happening? Don't react. Joseph was inside the dungeon, but he never let the dungeon get inside of him! How easily he could have become a prisoner to self-pity and seething resentment, or he could have dwelt on the incredible injustice that had resulted from the lies and false accusations of Potiphar's wife.

Joseph kept his heart pure and his conscience clean.

Are we modern Joseph's who watch people's faces, listen to their questions, and interpret their dreams and their nightmares? Do we in humility, but with authority, in tenderness, as well as courage, live out the Good News before others? Let's live out of our found-ness and fullness in Him?

Forgiveness

Another great thing about Joseph is that he learned to forgive completely from his heart. This is vitally important for us too. Jesus stressed forgiveness, *"If you forgive men their trespasses, your heavenly Father will also forgive you. But if you do not forgive men their trespasses, neither will your Father forgive your trespasses"* (Matt. 6:14-15). In other words, "do unto others as God in Christ has done unto you." *

So what is forgiveness?
- Forgiveness is the key relational issue of the Bible.
- Forgiveness must always come from our heart.
- Forgiveness brings deep inner healing.
- Forgiving is "facing" the specific wrong done to us.
- Forgiveness is facing our hurt and pain; facing the feelings that they caused in us. Don't deny the pain or injury. The wrongs and the feelings need to be connected.
- Forgiveness is also facing our resentments.

We must have the courage to face our real feelings toward the person before permanent healing or peace in the heart can begin. If you bury the hurts, you bury the hates. And if you bury the hurts and the hates, then you bury the possibility of finding healing (Eph. 4:25,31). We must "unfold the whole wretched story." *

After we have faced the wrongs and felt the hurts and admitted the resentments, there is only one place to go—the cross of Christ. *And be kind to one another, tenderhearted, forgiving one another, just as God in Christ forgave you* (Eph 4:32). Paul is saying that when God forgave us our sins through Christ's death, it was because God in Christ took onto

---

* This section on forgiving is from a sermon I gave at Eastwood. I read many resources and listened to several sermons to prepare for it, but didn't write them down. The words in quotes are from one of those unknown sources.

Himself and into Himself the guilt, the punishment, and the shame of our sins. These should have been ours because we deserved to suffer for them. Instead, God through Jesus took them into His very own being and by suffering for them was able to forgive us without overlooking or whitewashing our sins. He forgave us through "suffering love." *

All forgiveness involves "suffering love." Let's be honest. Let's begin where we are at! The hurt may be so great. But to be set free, we must go through with it. We must face it.

"Are you willing to be made willing?" We can ask for God's grace to help us get to where we are willing, even at the cost of greater pain. Let's choose that greater pain. God wants to give us new feelings. Let's accept the new feelings!

Ask yourself, "What would help me back to a new life?" This would: Obeying what the Lord's prayer says, *"Forgive us our sins as we forgive."* Forgiving sets us free! Free from past hurts. Free from unnecessary guilt, and condemnation. (There are necessary and unnecessary parts).

God's part: Get off God's turf! He will change the feelings and He will avenge. Let's stop breaking into the divine division of labor and stop trying to do what only God can do. We fallen human beings cannot really change our feelings about anything.

Our part: Give God permission to change us. Will and feelings are two different things. Let's let Jesus be Lord of both. The place of decision is a crisis of the will, where we decide to allow God to change us.

We have to confess our hurts and bitterness and truly forgive. We have to take full responsibility for ourselves and yield totally to the Spirit. We cannot disown our resentments until we own our responsibilities.

- Recall the source of bitterness—satan, the father of lies.
- Reiterate your will to forgive

* From my sermon, from one of those unknown sources.
(See page 87.)

- Refuse to allow guilt or condemnation a place in your heart.
- Remember God is faithful and will continue to change your feelings.
- Rejoice that God is pleased with you every step of the way.

God did this deep work in Joseph. He was mindful of Joseph's bitter memories. Joseph had a heart full of painful feelings. His eyes were overflowing with bitter tears. He had lived through twenty years of not seeing his brothers.

Joseph chose full forgiveness for them for the evil things they intentionally did to him. He forgave even when his feelings were overwhelming.

Can we thank and praise God for slowly and surely filling in the crannies and crevices of our hearts?

For Joseph, God thawed out his frigid heart, and gave him the grace to let others off the hook and restore them back into his life again. He received reconciliation.

Keep in mind, though, that forgiveness and reconciliation are not the same. Reconciliation requires humility and grace on both sides—Grace that says, "It's just you and me with no one to blame" and "I'm sorry" (Matt. 18:15).

There will not always be reconciliation. Your willingness for reconciliation doesn't mean it is guaranteed or always possible or advisable.

Don't expect better results than Jesus had. Forgiveness is a one-way street. Reconciliation is a two-way street! There are some no-win situations in life. Slow it down and wait on the Lord. Leave it up to His schedule and His timing. In the "fullness of time," God's plans come to pass. Continue praying for direction for your actions and the timing. Continue believing in God's power to harness evil and make it work to accomplish His purpose for our good and His glory. Joseph learned this (Gen. 50:20).

Here's the big picture: We Christians need the verse Genesis 50:20 *You meant evil against me; but God meant it for good.* We need this 50/20 vision to see that God is always at work making things turn out for His purpose. When evil seems so triumphant that we tend to become discouraged, we need to remember that God is indeed the Lord of history.

Taken from a sermon on Joseph by a minister friend of mine, Dr. Cheryl Piscipo.

Paul spoke of this too. Romans 8:28 is the over-arching providence of God in our lives. Our outlooks may change. Our convictions may sway, but *"the Scripture cannot be broken"* (John 10:35). And since it can't, since His Truth will not waver, since God's way will never alter, we can be sure that everything will work out for good. Joseph's pain had a purpose! His problems, struggles, heartaches, and hassles cooperated toward one end— the Glory of God. My prayer is that my own struggles will also.

The Immensity of God and Forgiveness
(Source unknown)

The <u>balance of truth,</u> which insists on an Almighty One working out His purposes and at the same time teaches that people through whom He works are <u>free agents,</u> has taxed the Lord's people for centuries. Joseph used two phrases which kept both sides of the truth before his brothers and also before us. On the one hand he told them, "You sold me," but at the same time he reminded them, "God sent me." In no way was their responsibility diminished but equally in no way had the Lord ever lost control of the situation.

The debate over Calvinism and Arminianism has waxed and waned over the years in the halls of ecclesiastical academia but out in the marketplace of life there are many who have resolved the problem for all practical purposes. They have learned from experience that to ignore the divine sovereignty is arrogance of the first degree but to ignore human accountability is irresponsibility on a grand scale.

Theologians will probably never finally figure out the mysteries of the divine will and the part that human decisions play in its outworking. I trust, however, that the Lord will hold a glorious seminar for us all in Glory when we can ask Him to finally sort these and other thorny subjects. Perhaps we should in the meantime join men like Joseph and others whose practical approach to the problem allowed them to continue in deep reverence and dependence while at the same time accomplishing much of significance through hard work and the proper utilization of divine gifts.

General William Booth, the founder of the Salvation Army, is a great example. He did not allow himself to be sidetracked in theological debate when he became aware of London's desperate and destitute masses. He put it all together when he insisted, "Work as if everything depended on your work and pray as if everything depended upon your prayer."

The story of Joseph and his brothers is so moving that it seems almost unreal. But when applied to our lives, it etches two unforgettable principles on our hearts. First, that God truly is in control and that He will ultimately prevail with or without the cooperation of His erring children. Second, when a man or a woman comes into contact with the immensity of God the result is a heart that pulsates with something of His love to such an extent that extraordinary depths of love and forgiveness flow from that grateful heart.

With all these wonderful things that Joseph did, one of the things he did the best was his attitude and faith at his death. He heard God and believed what God said all his life. At his death he

gave instructions concerning his bones, showing again his faith in God's promise that his people would return to the land.

Hearing God

I copied the following down from a study on the Book of Joshua and read it at a board meeting. They had been asking me about how to hear from God. That was years ago and I don't remember who the author was.

THERE IS AN ORACLE WHICH WILL WISELY GUIDE ALL WHO FEAR GOD: God has never been at a loss to guide the willing steps of men: but to the heart that has sought He has always given guidance. In various ways He has led men. Abraham through a whispering of His great name: Jacob and Joseph through dreams; Moses through voice and vision and miracle alike; Joshua through some gleaming of the high priest's breastplate; Gideon through the angel; Samuel through a raised state of faculty; the prophets by the breathings of great thoughts and feelings; Jonah's sailors by the lot; the wise men from the East by a star; the Ethiopian by a page of prophecy. He seems to accommodate all and give them their guidance where they expect to find it. God still "fulfils (sic) Himself" in many ways. ... The Moravians, who expect Divine guidance through the casting of the lot, doubtless find it there, though no one else would get it. Sometimes through a restraint like that which Paul described in the words "the spirit suffered us not"; sometimes through inward impulse of a cogent kind, a being "bound in the spirit to go" in a certain direction; sometimes by the mere commendation of certain courses to our taste, our judgment, or our conscience. God still gives guidance to all who ask it.

"Wait a minute. We've only got eight batters! We need nine."
The ninth one ain't even sure if he made the team. All he cares
about is that the children get to the Promised Land.

No one wants to bat last. But we've got a player on the team
that doesn't mind batting last. In fact, he said to God in God's
word (paraphrased), "God, I don't care if You bring me out, but
will You save Your promises to the other nations and save Your
people? I don't even care if I'm on the team!" He didn't care if he
batted last. You see, we have to understand as a church that each
one of us get a different call from God. We have to understand
our individual, personal call from our personal God. Because it
tells us in Hebrews 11:6 that we *can* please God. Most of us in
our life are choosing to please someone else. For most of us,
it's ourselves. We're trying to please ourselves. We must today
choose who we really want to please.

In Hebrews 11:6 it says there is one person you can please!
It is God! God can be pleased! Isn't that exciting? God can be
pleased. We please Him by faith. And He gives us the faith. How
can we go wrong? He gives us the grace to have the faith. And as
we apply and appropriate that faith, He will give us more! These
Hall of Faith men had this faith.

But our ball diamond is not complete. I've not said who plays
center field. We need a speedster. Who covered more land for
God than anyone else? Moses. He led the children of Israel to
the Promised Land. Center field is big. For center field you need
someone that can really cover the pasture. Who cares how they
can hit? It isn't just hitting. God's call for Moses was unique and
tough. Moses didn't want to do it. His call regarded choice.

They hid him as a baby for three months. Then along came
the princess and he had a chance. He had a chance to be one
of the greatest ever in Egypt. But he left all the riches and all the
best things of Egypt and took the worst of the believing life. He

chose to be on the team of those who suffered the most. It says it right there that he chose "to suffer affliction with" his mates.

He chose that over all the money and all the other things of Egypt. He had nothing going for him with these sore afflictions. But yet, he believed it was of God. And the key here is this. Every one of these people here in Hebrews 11 responded to the promises of God! Not their own. Of God! And they believed that God in His faithfulness to His promises would turn all for good; that you would be better off on that team than on the other team. And so he did it. He chose the people of God.

Oh, the choices he had to make. I started off saying I had to make some choices. I played center field where there are always choices to be made. Choices are hard. Life is hard. But the greatest choice we can make is to FIRST ASK, "What is God saying to us?" And respond. Respond in faith! And that will give us hope. Grace is of God. If it doesn't have grace in it, it's not God. It's just a religious spirit. Let's get back to grace. Let's get back to *being*. It's not by power or might. It's just being and believing. I had to learn that.

There is a lot of ground between us and God! And the great center fielder wants us to cover it in worship.

> Worship is a place of meeting between God— the Transcendent One—and the human creature. A strange place it is. There is acceptance but at the same tie, unworthiness. There is nearness but also distance. There is fear but also confidence. There is self awareness, yet there is God—all reality— between Creator and creature—is miraculously bridged.
>
> Worship, then, is the meeting place of divine interests and human need. To respect this double dimension is not easy. Too readily the worship settings become centered in the needs felt by

worshipers. The temptation is to assure that people *feel good* about the worship experience, and an element of entertainment is subtly introduced.

On the other hand, to focus on the divine side and the duty of worship without attention to the divine-human encounter inclines the worship toward traditionalism and formalism. In true worship we find our deepest human needs met in the same moment that we give absolute attention to God. To touch God is to be touched by God.

Taken from "Worship Is Holy Ground" from the *EMC Bulletin* of Eastern Mennonite College & Seminary.

The great center fielder finds balance to connect. God gives the Signal!! "What do you suppose God wants? Choose God's face. Hear His call to where your place is on the team. The pitch is God's. God has one goal: to bring us into His glory and to show His glory to the world (Isaiah 66:18, John 17:24).

Moses took on the spirit and attitude of the people and hit the rock twice. The best, most humble, meekest man on earth struck out and was not allowed to enter the Promised Land. Yet he is in the Hall of Faith. God extended grace to him. There is hope for us.

You see, every one of these people has a unique word behind them, God showed me. That blew my mind when I woke up. God showed me that Abel's main call was sacrifice. Enoch's main call was walk—a walk of faith. Noah's was a gift of grace—that grace will clean up everything. Great exploits come in grace. If we think it's not grace, they will not come. Abraham's great call was a call of obedience. These are key words. Each one had something. Moses' was choice. He had to choose. History said it was destined of him to be in charge. He had to choose to leave all the moneys of Egypt—all the wealth—all the power—all the

prestige. He chose to suffer the afflictions of his brothers—his teammates. He could've been on the other team. But he chose to be on this team. This team looked like it would never win.

I've played softball with some teams that when we started off in the beginning of the year, I didn't think they'd ever win. It isn't always who's got the best players. It's who's got the best heart and the best spirit, isn't it? And those teams that respond to the call and work as a team usually find a way to win. Those are the churches that lay their foundations in grace and are gracious to God, themselves, and others. Those are the teams and churches that will win. Moses chose the right team.

Moses also chose faith. God gave him the faith to go through the Red Sea. God may have called you and given you the faith to go through your Red Sea. Others He has called to do other things. We had better not try to go through a sea if God hasn't called us to do that.

We have choices today. We have choices of how we will respond to the grace of God; to the faith He has given; to the call He's given us; to the call He has given others. God is looking for people today who will play different positions. The former team has died and gone on and God is looking for new players. And God's Word says that we can do more than them—more than them!! In Him! Not ourselves. I don't know in what area your hope needs to be rebuilt. It doesn't matter. If you believe that God is God and is the rewarder of them that believe in Him, it will happen. The Scripture says we must believe that He is—that He is! That HE is, not someone else, not you are, not something else is. God is! Our faith is built on the foundation that He is!

Also God is a rewarder. Oh, I've had people tell me that God does not reward. I want to tell you that is a lie from the pit of hell. Some say there are no rewards in following God. Yes, there are. Noah's family was saved. Joseph's family was saved. The

Word of God says our God is a rewarder of them that diligently seek Him. If you will choose to continue to seek Him and believe that He will reward you—in time—His time—He WILL reward you. Those are His promises! I woke up that morning and I had to make a new choice like Moses. I had to believe. Is my God really who He says He is? I had to lose confidence in myself and confidence in others—in everyone else—including our family, including my mother! That doesn't mean my mother was bad. But everyone, I don't care who: mother, father, brothers, sisters, ourselves, everyone else—is not God! We have to hear from God ourselves. God is God!! I had to make a decision that day that HE IS; and that because there would be NEW rewards, I could go on. I could forget the past. It was too much—too overwhelming. But God gave me a new faith that I could get back up and be more nobly rebuilt. We can be more nobly rebuilt in the Spirit of God today, in God's grace. Those are the foundations of the call of who the church is. The church is the Bride of Christ—not based on how good we are, but on how good He is.

By the way, just a side note, Sarah made the team. She's not playing today, but she's there. Her faith is there too. She was mentioned along with Abraham. All her faith came when she laughed about it. "Huh? We're having a baby?" Some laugh that women play on the team.

Sarah was good. But Sarah was not good because of Sarah. Sarah was not good because of her faithfulness. Sarah was good because of God's grace. The Holy Spirit showed me that Sarah was good because of the faithfulness of her God. Hebrews 11:11b says this: Sarah's faithfulness was in God's faithfulness.

The Bible says we've all sinned. Let's quit judging that they're sins are worse than our sins. The Bible says we have all sinned. That's why David is the catalyst of this team. That's why God started off with David!! David knew how sinful he was. And

97

our team will not start off until we have a lead-off catalyst who can get on base and know how sinful they are.

Sarah knew that her God was faithful. Even though she was of old age, that God could restart a barren soul. Is there anything we limit God in? Well, let's make sure it's of God, not our own call. The key is: Is it God's call or our call? If it's our call, it's presumptuous. If it's God's call, there are no limitations. But Sarah finally made the team. Oh, by the way, Rahab also did—a harlot—a prostitute! She's on the team! God chooses all kinds from all backgrounds for His team.

There is a story that's told about four men who played poker all night long and toasted the winner after each deal. Finally morning came and the party broke up; but as they were headed for home, they heard church bells ringing and began to feel guilty that they had spent the entire night gambling and drinking. So they decided to go to church. Still not altogether sober, they sang with the fervor found at any good drinking party. When the offering was taken, they sought penance by each dropping a $100 dollar bill in the plate. After the service was over, the pastor, being a bit puzzled about the visitors, asked the head usher if he knew the gentlemen. The usher said, "No, I've never seen them before. However, they sang like United Methodists alright, but they gave like Roman Catholics and smelled like Episcopalians."

I have often wondered, wouldn't it be grand to serve a church that had all the best qualities of the other denominations and none of the worst?

… Too often we look across the narrow ditches that separate us and ignore the common, solid ground we all stand on.

Taken from: *Circuit Rider* May 1991, Vol. 1, No. 4, copyright 1991, by the United Methodist Publishing House (ISBN 0146-9924). Written by Editor, Keith I. Pohl.

Let us learn from all of our teammates. We need all kinds. The critical question the Gospel poses to the church is not, "Are you charismatic?" or "Are you fundamental?" or "Are you a liberal?" or "Are you a conservative?" but rather "Will you take up your cross and follow Him?" The core issue is radical, nonjudgmental discipleship! Will we see our teammates through His eyes of mercy and compassion and serve them as He did?

A Living Bible
Author Unknown

His name is Bill. He has wild hair, wears a T-shirt with holes in it, jeans, and no shoes. This was literally his wardrobe for his entire four years of college. He is brilliant. Kind of esoteric and very, very bright. He became a Christian while attending college.

Across the street from the campus is a well-dressed, very conservative church. They want to develop a ministry to the students, but are not sure how to go about it. One day Bill decides to go there. He walks in with no shoes, jeans, his T-shirt, and wild hair. The service has already started, so Bill starts down the aisle looking for a seat. The church is completely packed and he can't find a seat. By now people are really looking a bit uncomfortable, but no one says anything. Bill gets closer and closer and closer to the pulpit and, when he realizes there are no seats, he just squats down right on the carpet. [Although perfectly acceptable behavior at a college fellowship, trust me, this had never happened in this church before!]

By now the people are really uptight, and the tension in the air is thick. About this time, the minister realizes that from way at the back of the church, a deacon is slowly making his way toward Bill. Now the deacon is in his eighties, has silver-gray hair, and a three-piece suit. A Godly man, very elegant, very dignified, very courtly, he walks with a cane. And as

he starts walking toward this boy, everyone is saying to themselves that you can't blame him for what he's going to do. How can you expect a man of his age and of his background to understand some college kid on the floor?

It takes a long time for the deacon to reach the boy. The church is utterly silent except for the clicking of the man's cane. All eyes are focused on him. You can't even hear anyone breathing.

The minister can't even preach the sermon until the deacon does what he has to do. And now they see this elderly man drop his cane on the floor. With great difficulty he lowers himself and sits down next to Bill and worships with him so he won't be alone.

Everyone chokes up with emotion. When the minister gains control, he says, "What I'm about to preach, you will never remember. What you have just seen, you will never forget. Be careful how you live. You may be the only Bible some people will ever read."

How can we judge others when we ourselves are messes needing to constantly choose to be washed in Jesus' Blood? A young woman in my congregation wrote a poem illustrating our weaknesses very well. She was given an assignment in her college psychology class to write twenty "I am" statements about herself. She wrote to me, "That poor atheist professor got a little more than he bargained for! I even titled it for him! Honestly, I think it was a witness to him. You'd be surprised by the respect I got from him when he handed it back to me. The real blessing that came out of this, though, is how the Lord showed me that within myself there is no stability. It's only by centering myself on Him that there is any stability. ... I actually lost some of what might be considered overconfidence by acknowledging I'm nothing that's worth anything without the Lord. He's my only real center and only when His work in me is done will I actually BE anything."

I Am a Paradoxical Phenomenon

By Marcy Mietz

I am a born-again Christian infatuated with science
I am a scientist consumed by spiritual truth

I am a saint who will do anything for anyone
I am a faithless sinner wholly dependent on a merciful God

I am a best friend, counselor and "quicker picker upper"
I am a recluse rejuvenated by the silence of solitude

I am a devout fan of logic, guided by emotion
I am an emotional wreck who despises my logic

I am a realist who dares to dream the impossible dream
I am a dreamer with feet planted firmly in reality

I am a heavenly creation that I swear was a joke
I am the comedian who chooses to continue the tradition

I am easily amused, which may be quite evident
I am extremely hard to please, which is much less so

I am a seeker who knows the best way to hide
I am the most honest person to ever tell a lie

I am a perfectionist left wallowing in my own imperfection
I am a control freak who acknowledges my utter lack of control

I am a mass of confusion who's got it all figured out
I am open for interpretation without a doubt

I am not simply A or even B or C
I am all of the above unapologetically

*D*o you want to get on the team? I don't care what your past has been. I don't even care where you are now. In faith, all that matters is if God's Spirit has called you and said, "Come! I invite you! Come! You can be on the team!" Our job as the church is to be the salt and the light, to go out and tell. The church is for those yet not in us. We are to go out and appeal. Not us doing it

101

in our force, but the power of the sweet Holy Spirit and grace—appealing. Come. You can be a part of us, unless you're perfect. If you're perfect, please don't come here. You will mess us up. We'll start thinking it's because of our goodness and righteousness.

By the way, Abel was witnessed by God that he was righteous—righteous in God's grace. Also, for some of the others, it was witnessed of them that they pleased God and God smiled on them. Are you more concerned with the smile of God or of the smile of someone else? Are you more concerned with your own smile of satisfaction regarding possessions or God's smile? Are you, with your conscience, bearing good witness? I had no hope because my conscience didn't bear me good witness. But the conscience can be rebuilt. It can have the witness of God that I can start over. "My grace is sufficient for the day thereof." And that day is now!!

Do you want your conscience rebuilt? It can be rebuilt today by the Spirit of God, by God's grace. That is the message of the church. Those are the new foundations that God wants to lay in His church. That is what God is calling us to be—to be for Him in faith. New foundations of grace, not us, not what we can be, not our dreams, not our will, but His dreams, His will, His wisdom, His way! His way is grace!

The Word of God says our righteousness "is as filthy rags." Let's get our eyes off our own righteousness and on the righteousness of Christ in faith. And when we respond and receive and appropriate that in faith, God will do great exploits. When we sacrifice ourselves, our will, our ways, our positions, our choices, then God comes in with His time and His way. Then there are exploits when He chooses. And He usually does it for the weakest. He picks which one will swing away. Abraham was a free swinger. When he swung, he had no idea where the ball was going. He didn't even know where *he* was going. Then there are others that were pure hitters. When Enoch hit the ball, he knew exactly where it was going. Every hitter swings different. Some swing left, some swing right. Some hit the ball a short distance. Some hit it long distances. It doesn't matter. Let's quit deciding. God has given the call for all people from the world to come into the church. Let's quit judging which positions. There are positions for all—for all that join God's team. This is a message that will go all over the world. This is a call from God to join God's team. God made the decision. God made the call.

We need to choose to have an attitude of thanksgiving toward God. The people Moses lead were whining, complaining, grumbling people. God hated their attitude so much, He left their bones in the desert. It is faith and an attitude of thanksgiving and grace that pleases God.

Do you want to play ball? God's way is a joy way. It's not a hard way. Religion is a hard way. Oh my preaching was so hard. I used to brag how hard it was. But God's way is the easy way, the light way, the joyous, adventurous way. It's exciting! God gives the adventure! Praise God, it's great!!

We can join God's team. Do you want to? However God has spoken to you today, will you receive it? Different people will respond in different ways to you—to how you decide. Who's your main audience? Is it God or them? Is it God or yourself? Who's the judge? Who's the captain? Who are the coaches? "But I can't do that!" You're right. You can't. Unless the Holy Spirit is working in you and through you, and is equipping you, you will not hit home plate and score. Even in ministry! That's grace.

*L*et's choose to believe in God's grace so we can be winners. Take your sins to the cross. When you sin, draw in to God. That's the time to draw in, in grace. And encourage others to. Don't tell them to try harder. Don't try harder. I tried harder. I told others to try harder. It isn't the answer. Grace is. Are you grounded in

God's grace? Will you encourage others to ground there? Put your faith in God's grace. That's our call. That's our choice.

God called Moses to choose. He called me that day, "Choose, Art." Has my life been perfect since then? No. I've made a lot of mistakes. I knew I would. I told Him I would. "That's okay, Art. My love will not change." I want you to play again. And this time don't worry about whether you blow it or make an error. But, in your heart, in your will, I want you to lift up your mind to Me. I want you to lift up your action, your will to Me. Consistently put yourself in My promises. Put your confidence and your assurance in My grace. That will be the change, Art. That will be the start.

God does His most stunning work where things seem hopeless. Wherever there is pain, suffering, and desperation, Jesus is. And that's where His people belong, among those who are vulnerable, who think nobody cares. What better way for the brilliance of Christ to shine?

Lovingly and forcefully, God called me to look in the mirror of God, to repent of all my futile attempts to do the work of the Holy Spirit. I desired to have my voice worth hearing again. I wanted a passion and a purity that brings force and clarity to the grand old Gospel—bringing it alive with contemporary vitality and beauty. The main requirement was to be natural and sincere.

His word to me was grounded in countless promises repeated in the Scriptures. It was the very thing that had produced every revival of the Holy Spirit throughout history. God was now drawing me, pulling me toward an actual experience of Himself and His power. If we call upon the Lord, He has promised in His Word to answer, to bring the unsaved to Himself, to pour out His Spirit among us.

I've started again. How far I'll go, I don't know. It will depend on how much I believe in God's grace. It's the same for you. I can do all things through Christ who strengthens me. Paul found grace. I want to find it. I want you to find it. Not performance. Not great exploits. The exploit has been done at the cross! It's grace!

That should be the greatest exploit that we're praying for. For what we seek we shall find. What we ask, we shall get. The door we knock on will be opened to us. That was my cry. That was what I was seeking, that was what I was asking. Grace was what I was knocking for—it was what I wanted to be opened to me. And now I no longer care how others criticize how I worship. I want to worship God with my whole heart. God says if I seek Him, He is a rewarder. He's my main audience.

I needed a transformation. I needed to be rebuilt. I needed new hope. I needed new faith. I needed grace! No one else could give it to me. I couldn't give it to myself. "God, give me your grace! " I said. "God, You're going to have to change my whole personality." He's been doing that, but He's not done yet.

What is God saying to you today? You worship. You respond. You receive. You apply. You appropriate it in the way the Spirit of God has spoken to you today. Will you do it personally? We have a personal God, which is good. You can please God. There are lots of people you can't please, but you can please God today.

In the closing verses of Hebrews 11, the writer describes the range of experiences of those living by faith—closing the mouths of lions, receiving their dead back to life, victorious in battle, being tortured, beaten, imprisoned, even being brutally killed. *All of these people we have mentioned received God's approval because of their faith, yet none of them received all that God had promised. 40 For God had far better things in mind for us that would also benefit them, for they can't receive the prize at the end of the race until we finish the race* (Heb. 11:39-40 NLT).

So, let's finish the race—for their sake as well as for our own sake!

God gave me comfort and showed me that He has forgiven me for my failures through amazing Father's Day poems and letters from my kids. Here's one Kelson wrote in 2008 (shortened to fit here).

DAD

Thank you for:
- teaching me how to be athletic and perform
- teaching me how to be ok being outside the Norm
- always believing in me
- always motivating me to be more than what I thought I could be

Thank you for:
- being passionate, persistent, and driven in what you want me to see
- your sense of humor, for it has rubbed off on me to laugh freely
- your sincerity, it truly is admirable to experience as many have said
- your compassion for the weak ... and showing them how to be led

Thank you for continuing:
- to grow as a person, showing me we all can grow when we choose to
- to learn ... showing ... we can always learn [something] new ...
- to stay consistent in your love for God ... an example to look through
- [in] your honesty to show me ... to be forthright thru and thru

Thank you for your:
- enduring efforts to become a better person, YOU HAVE for all to see
- patience when I was not a true example of God's love
- spirit, as it is becoming more at peace each year, you are truly a success
- knowledge, wisdom, and discernment, the truest form of God's love from above

Chapter 4

Relaunched

Spring Training

There's a baseball saying about our past mistakes and flub ups: We've got to put it behind us, build off it, and do everything we can to make sure it doesn't happen again. People have got to learn to put the past behind them. There are even team psychiatrists to help players learn how to move through their mistakes and learn from them, not to dwell on them too much.

It is not just errors that can set you back. Too many successes can also become a problem. Reporters asked Rod Carew, one of the greatest hitters, what his hardest AB (at bat) was. He said it was his fifth time to bat after he had four straight hits. He said it was too tempting to take it easy and to not concentrate on the fifth hit. Never give up an AB!

Every team goes over all the basics again every year during spring training. They don't just rest on their past successes. Each team after the winter lay-off, goes over the basics first. They repeat basic plays twenty or thirty times to make sure they get it right. The inner thought is: If I go over the basics again, I can do better next time. They do the same for their weaknesses—so they won't trip them up again. Then they go over new ideas.

They don't want to lose what they've got. They go through the training with goals in mind. They want to do their best. They work harder in training than at any time. It's like going through fire.

For outfield training, they work hard learning to back each other up, making sure each player is in the right position when the

107

ball comes. They have to learn how and where to shift depending on whether the ball comes, for example, toward third base or first base. For each type of hit or throw or for cut-off plays, the players have to learn where to go. Each one has to be in the right position at the right time, ready to back each other up for the sake of the team. We don't want spectators on the field, we want participators.

Batting practice includes drills on bunting, hitting, and running. Field training includes drills on throwing and on learning things like what is best to do in a rundown. Players get themselves in the best possible condition so they can do their best that season. You don't have to be perfect to be a good batter. You don't have to bat 1000. 300 is good. That means the most professional hitter misses 7 out of 10 times. An average player hits 1 out of 4. Team batting average is 250. Only about ten players per year have an over 300 average. God goes by the heart of it.

Baseball is all about adjustments, and adjustments to the adjustments! The Lord showed me I had major holes in my baseball swing. The adjustments of grace and also the boundary issues need a lot of maturity. Developing discipline not to swing at pitches outside the strike zone and to not over swing is not easy. Short, quick swings to the center of the ball are what bring good hits. We have to stop getting ahead of God. We need to be careful not to over swing or over throw. We need to follow His eyes beholding Jesus and know that He has the power to produce in RBI situations. Let Him always lead. Follow close and believe that He will deliver and come through in the clutch. God can blow the winds of momentum at any time. No matter what the score or what inning; it's not over till the 27th out. God knows how to rally and He desires that you and I have a part in the victory!

In spring training, one guy may not make the team. Many of the 25 team members are extra players. Still they go through the

training just like everyone else. Some players train for three or four different positions, not knowing whether they will be chosen or not. You need to be ready to submit to the managers and coaches decisions.

Pitchers

Now let's take a look at pitchers and see what things about pitching we can apply to our spiritual lives. I have been a pitcher since I was a kid. One thing that affects pitching is the wind. When the wind is blowing, as a pitcher, I'm going to adjust myself to it. I will try to make the best use of the power of that wind. The wind determines how the pitches are going to flow that day. The Spirit is the wind. Am I adjusting to Him or He to me?

I was one of those people who said I just go by the Word. But the Holy Spirit wrote the Word and speaks a lot about Himself in the Word. The Word says that God sent Jesus and Jesus sent the Holy Spirit. I am learning that no outward teaching can replace the inward power of the Holy Spirit. I'm no longer alone running and running. The Holy Spirit is in me.

I know there are misgivings about the Holy Spirit and those that misuse the gifts. What happens when we don't adjust to the wind? We must adjust to God; not God to us. The answer is flowing in the power of the Holy Spirit and the grace of God, not in our own carnal ideas. We must be Spirit-filled and Spirit-controlled and we must keep on being filled.

The strike zone is 17 inches wide (the width of home plate) and the height is approximately from the batter's knees to his mid chest. Pitchers miss the strike zone lots of times. It is dangerous to miss it. A batter can be seriously injured. The width is almost the same length as from our mind to our heart (depending on our height, of course). In our lives, we can miss the strike zone—the heart of us. We make most of our decisions out of our minds, but

our minds must be renewed. We must put the heart part—the part connected to God—first.

We should listen to our heart part—our inner voice. God took the deepest part of His Spirit and put it in us. Part of it is our conscience—our "knower." We must be in touch with our knower. We know deep in our knower when we have pitched to the strike zone and when we have missed it.

Pitching is not only about the velocity and speed, but also the stance, poise, and command. This is symbolic of our spiritual character. It all works best when God calls the pitches.

A good pitcher covers both sides of the plate when he pitches. I'm afraid people are not covering both sides of the plate—the humanity and the divinity of Christ or predestination versus free choice—some are on one side and some on the other. Scripture is full of examples of imbalance to one side or the other. The call now is to encourage and support each other, understanding the balance of Christ in the power of the Holy Spirit to the Glory of God. I don't have all the answers on these or other controversial things, but I know the One who does!

In baseball they say a team is no better than its pitching. Pitching is everything. On a major league roster of 25 players on the team, 12-14 are pitchers. Most are relief pitchers. They don't pitch until deep into the game, maybe not until the sixth inning. The starting five pitchers pitch every fifth day. There is usually a long reliever pitcher and a couple that are good at strike outs, maybe due to a good sinker ball pitch they have. There are special left-handed pitchers for left-handed batters, and one pitcher might be just for the ninth inning. These extra pitchers have to spend most of the game time on the bench. They all know where their fit is. They know why they are there. They will be brought out when the game is on the line and they are needed for their special skills or when their team is ahead by a few runs.

But they aren't useless to the team there in the dugout. They don't just waste their bench time. They use it to cheer the other players on, giving encouragement and lifting spirits when needed.

There are special hitters on a team too. On one team it was an older guy who couldn't run well, but he could bat home runs. They called him out when they had to get the runs in. His job was just to sit and wait for the special moments when they called on him.

Everyone knows that as a team you will go as far as your pitching takes you. We have the Big Three pitching to us. They have always won and have never lost. They finish what they start. They complete games. They pitch with perfect poise and command. (This game is not like ordinary baseball games. In our game of life, the enemy never pitches to us. In our spiritual baseball, God is in control of everything that comes our way.)

I believe the Big Three have three perfect pitches that are exemplified in Isaiah 40:31 (KJV) *But they that wait upon the LORD shall renew their strength; they shall mount up with wings as eagles; they shall run, and not be weary; and they shall walk, and not faint.*

1. The Fastball

When we hit God's fast pitch, our ball rises high into the air and becomes a home run. *"They shall mount up with wings as eagles."* Flying like eagles is obviously not something people can do, so this represents the miraculous intervention of God. It's the answer from God all of us long for in the face of our problems. To mount up on wings, we must be focused on the Lord and in tune to what He is sending our way—sensitive to what He is telling us to do.

2. The Curve Ball

For the curve pitch, we need to be even more tuned in to our Father. When you hit the curve ball dead on, it becomes

a long drive. If we run fast, we will be able to make it around the bases. Running without growing weary is representative of cooperating with God in whatever unexpected curve he sends us—cooperating in ways that solve our problems.

3. The Change-Up

Another pitch image is of walking without fainting. This represents God's presence with us in endurance. It is the answer to problems that we least prefer, yet God is often at work in these situations in ways that are beyond our immediate understanding. These are the "My grace is enough" moments in life. We simply put one foot in front of the other and keep walking the journey, dark and painful as it may be.

I'm thankful I don't have to figure all this out for God's baseball team. I'm glad He takes care of everything—the spring training, the team members assignments, the line-ups, the coaching, the pitching, etc! I'm glad He knows exactly what's needed for us to win the game! The question is, "Do I trust God? Do I have faith in His calls? Do I have faith that He will qualify those he chooses?"

Ball Players Today that Are on God's Team

In the middle of the year in baseball, people vote for the All-Star players. God sent us His second-chance gift in Jesus. Are we going to come to the place where we know that we can't make it on our own? Are we going to accept God's second-chance gift? We vote by accepting Him.

Let's learn from a few baseball players of today who have accepted Him. God is using them to further His Kingdom. We can also be on this team of life. There are still many spots open.

Frank Robinson was the first black baseball manager. In 1975 his Cleveland Indians team was taking on the Yankees. On opening day, with 75,000 fans watching, he pinched hit himself

in the ninth inning and had a two-run homer. I remember this game. There was a snowstorm during the game. I drove a couple hours in that wintry weather to be there for this historical day.

<u>Orel Hershiser</u> is a pitcher hall of famer. In 1988, he broke a record, pitching 59 innings straight with no scores. In 1989, as a pitcher, he was the highest paid player in the history of baseball. In 1991, he returned to pitching baseball after shoulder reconstruction surgery, a recovery that no pitcher before him had ever accomplished. He gave God all the glory for his recovery. He is no longer a ball player today, but is an expert on baseball. He does sports analysis. He is a catalyst today for the Kingdom of God through his writing. He has written articles (including "Trust" in *Focus on the Family,* July 2002) and books (including *Between the Lines*) to help draw people to the Lord.

<u>Shawn Green</u> is a Jewish man. There was controversy about whether he would decide to play on the highest Jewish holy day—Yom Kippur (Day of Atonement). He was a great player. If he didn't play it made a big difference. He chose not to play. He decided there are some things more important than how his baseball did in that play-off game. Doing this caused other people to stop and consider what are the most important things in life.

<u>Bill Buckner</u> is a renowned ball player, but in 1986, he made a fielding error that cost the Red Sox the World Series. It was played up big in the news. He vowed he would never go out on the stadium again. But in 2008 he was asked to go out and throw the first pitch. In order to do that, he had to forgive the media for what they put him and his family through.

How about you? Do you have people you need to forgive?

<u>Mike Piazza</u> and <u>Pedro Martinez</u> hated each other, but then they were free agents to be on the same team. They chose to put the past behind them and treat each other like teammates.

Is there a Christian brother or sister you need to make amends with and begin to treat them like the teammate that they are in the Kingdom of Heaven?

Roberto Alomar was an allstar player. He was one of the best second basemen ever. But during one game he spit in the face of an umpire. People turned on him. The media gossip roared. This caused his proud father a lot of pain.

Later that umpire after avoiding Alomar in games, made the first move to patch things up. Since then Alomar has made very large donations and held successful fundraisers for finding a cure for a rare brain disease that the umpire's son has. Alomar and his brother, also a baseball player, have been donating autographed jerseys for charity auctions and hosting golf tournaments near their hometown.

Vladimer Guerrera is a tremendous hitter. He swings at everything and he hits it all! People love him. He always gives thanks to God by pointing to the sky. It is his signature pose.

Are we giving God the credit and the praise like Vladimer does? God is looking for new players with thankful attitudes.

Brett Gardner is a Yankee speedster. He's one of the fastest runners on the Yankees and in all of baseball. One day on a hospital visit, he met a teen girl waiting for a heart transplant who told him she had prayed for him to hit a homer that day. He wasn't even in the line-up, but in the third inning, he was asked to pinch hit. At his second at bat, he hit an inside-the-park homer, a rare thing in baseball. He made it home because of his speed. That was a miracle, but the greater miracle, for which he had prayed, was that she had a successful heart transplant that same evening. (Taken in part from "Allyssa's Homer" by Brett Gardner, *Guide Post,* October 2010)

David Freese in 2011 had the best performance in the play-offs and in the World Series and was named MVP (most valuable player). He also won the 2009 World Series, but soon afterwards was in a car accident. This was the third time he had been badly hurt. He was on crutches for awhile, had to take extended times off the field for recovery, including for three separate surgeries. But he persevered and God brought him back. God gave him favor. Let this encourage you to persevere when you have set backs and interruptions in your life. Trust God that He will also give you favor in your calling.

Albert Pujols has been a National League MVP twice. He is the only player in history to hit more than 30 home runs in each of his first eight seasons. He goes to church, repeatedly mentions his devotion to God, raises money for children with Down Syndrome in the USA, and goes on mission trips to help the poor in his native Dominican Republic. ... Pujols says, "I've always had the responsibility to God to be a role model .... I play to represent God, something bigger than baseball. This is not about me. I leave everything up to God." (Taken from "Faith Compels Pujols to Help Less Fortunate" by Mel Antonen, *USA TODAY*, 3/31/2009.)

Here's one radio talk show host's opinion about players like Albert Pajols who give visible petition and glory to God during games.

War on Religious Gestures (in sports)

Why should religious leaders, of all people, turn their fire on celebrities who use their popularity for public proclamations of the Almighty's power? In an age when media icons flaunt every sort of indulgence and depravity, [we] should find more appropriate targets to scold than athletic achievers like football's Tim Tebow, basketball's Jeremy Lin or baseball's Josh Hamilton [and Albert Pujols], who choose to flaunt their devout Christian commitment. ...

When Christian sports figures point toward the clouds or drop to their knees in prayer, they merely express gratitude for the Lord's grace and generosity in allowing them to perform at the peak of their abilities. ... [E]xpressions of appreciation to a higher power help place even our silliest earthly endeavors in proper perspective. ... When the most

admired public figures take time to express gratitude and share credit, it suggests an admirable quality of humility that remains in short supply in celebrity culture and the nation at large.

Michael Melved, *USA TODAY,* 7/9/2012

<u>Josh Hamilton</u> Moving forward after his brush with relapse, Rangers' outfielder, Josh Hamilton looks to improve his game both on and off the field. He was the No. 1 pick from high school in 1999 and went on to be the best player in baseball. But no one from his family could be around him and he got into drugs. His team took a chance on him and allowed him back. Then he had two more relapses. He was shut out of baseball for three years. After that officials gave him yet another chance on the condition that he have an accountability partner go with him everywhere.

Hamilton has let the world know that he has become a believer. The year he returned, I (Art Zehr, the author) prophesied that Hamilton would be one of the best players. No one had much confidence in him, but he surprised them all, hitting 18 home runs in one of the sectionals of the MLB All-Star home run contest. Yes he has had relapses since, but God has blessed him and shown him favor because he has shown his scars to the world. Drug addicts flock to see him because he gives them hope. (Read his book, *Beyond Belief: Finding the Strength To Come Back.*)

Are we asking God to help us with our past and our weaknesses?

Since Hamilton's last relapse, the Ranger's general manager, Jon Daniels, confirmed that Hamilton will face no discipline from the team or MLB. Daniels told the Dallas morning news, "We will take additional steps to support him."

I believe we could learn some things from baseball on encouraging and supporting people. I know in my life I have gotten more encouragement and support from baseball than from churches. I thought churches were to preach Good News! What are we preaching? Laws, rules, policies, and performance! The Bible teaches that when we judge ourselves we need no other judgment (I Cor. 11:31). Let's get on the diamond of grace.

I know the diamond of grace has laws, rules, policies and performances in it. For example, if you bat out of turn in baseball, you make an out. I believe most churches are batting out of turn! Is that why there is not much joy and praise in most churches? Let's quit making out-of-turn outs, and let God, the owner and manager, give us the batting order as he did in Hebrews 11. Salvation showcases God's mercy. It makes nothing of our efforts, but everything of His. He asks us to take care of the House, not take over the House!! (This is either a reminder or a reprimand, whichever fits.) Let's extend grace and have fun playing ball on God's team. I hope He gives you an "Atta boy!" or "Atta girl!"

In my years of waiting on God to fulfill the rest of my dream, I was worshiping and communing with God, letting God shape me and cleanse my spirit and do those heart operations that only the Holy Spirit can do. I read the Bible through five times the first year after my dream. I was profoundly stirred and, to be honest, disturbed. The apostles had this instinct: when in trouble, pray. When intimidated, pray. When challenged, pray. When persecuted, pray.

Today, several years after my baseball dream encounter, I know who I am! I now have a full measure of the peace, joy and wisdom of God. I BELONG on the team because He created, called and chose me to be on the team. God believes in me and thinks I can help the spiritual Kingdom church ball team!

I now know for sure that God loves me. To *not* know that we are loved is to live without a sense of true BELONGING in the world. When we have no sense of BELONGING, we are prone to live without appropriate boundaries, to overreach, and to desire things that distract us from our calling.

Paul's single-minded focus on the spread of the Gospel enabled him to not allow personal comfort and agenda to so define him that he lost sight of what he was called to be and do. He writes, *"I have learned to be content with whatever I have. I know what it is to have little and I know what it is to have plenty"* (Phil. 4:11-12 NIV) *"I have suffered the loss of all things, and count them as rubbish, that I may gain Christ"* (Phil. 3:8).

But it must be noted here that these two passages of Scripture have been subject to abuse. It is a poor use of Paul's words here to support bad habits that we may have developed over time. Paul was testifying to a personal discipline, not inviting us to abuse ourselves or others by living unhealthy lives.

I want a great many things I haven't got, but I don't want them enough to be discontent. True contentment deals openly and honestly with our hopes and dreams but refuses to let any desire snatch peace and joy from us.

Bernice

A few weeks after my dream, I attended a meeting held by a pastor lady, Bernice. She preached on singles and said something so pointedly true that it shocked me. She declared, "You date for only one of two reasons. You either want to take them to bed or to the altar."

Now, I had a prejudice against women church leaders, so I tried to get away right after the meeting, but God prevented me. A guy I'd sold a car to stopped me and said, "You've got to meet Bernice." As soon as Bernice heard my name, she said, "I heard you on the radio! I loved the mediating you were doing for singles." Then she said something very out of the ordinary. "God wants you in the ministry because you have felt pain. I had a dream about you. God told me that with what you have gone through you will know how to minister to others."

This really shook me up. She was talking about the very thing for which I believed God could never use me. She continued, "In your weakest area, this is where God is going to use you for this time—for this season."

I found out that she was a pastor of a very large church. She had said, "I'll be the pastor until God sends a man." When the church got to a 1000 members and there still wasn't a man, she accepted that her call was to continue pastoring. She says many poignant things. One of them is, "Any area we're reacting in, we're not dead yet." She also says we need to quit hiding our sins.

After I had the dream, I preached the sermon that weekend three times just as God had said I would. I was then invited to preach it at other places for the following two weeks and then there was nothing. I was puzzled. "God, what's happening?"

Well, it wasn't long afterwards that I met Bernice. Then later I got a call from her asking me to start a singles ministry at her church, Faith Tabernacle. I attended her church awhile to get established. Then we organized the ministry. We called it Faith Singles and met every Saturday night. The first night we thought we might get 20 or 30 people. We got 68! I lead it successfully from 1988 to 1993. Bernice was like an Abraham to me, She modeled to me how to hear God, and how to catch God's vision. She became like a spiritual mother to me.

Next I worked four years as a full-time evangelist for "In His Presence Ministry in Bay City, MI. While I was there, the Women's Center asked me to facilitate a seminar. (See brochure on the following pages.)

Family Violence

A Religious Response

April 19, 2001
9:00am - 3:00pm
Hereford and Hops
Banquet Room
804 E Midland St.
Bay City, MI

Sponsored by the
Bay Area Women's Center

Agenda

8:30—9:00am
Registration

9:00am
Welcome

9:10am-11:30am
*"Broken Vows"-
Video
Discussion follow-
ing: Pastor Art
Zehr-facilitator*

11:30am-12:45pm
*Luncheon with
Keynote Address by
Pastor Roger Lyman*

1:00pm-2:00pm
*"Hear Their Cries"
-Video Discussion
following: Amy
Hendrix-Facilitator*

2:30pm-3:00pm
*Closing Remarks and
Benediction*

What is this seminar about?

This seminar is about how churches and synagogues can better respond to the issue of family violence. The materials presented over the course of this day-long seminar will represent an interdenominational approach to discussing family violence within your congregations, what the church can do to support survivors of family violence and how to answer questions your congregation may have about different issues such as forgiveness, restoration of the family and safety. You will also have the chance to hear from many leaders within the Presbyterian, Baptist, Catholic, Evangelical and Jewish faiths about their own understanding of these issues.

You Will Learn about...

- What family violence is.
- What kind of spiritual support survivors of family violence need.
- How to identify different types of family violence.
- How to educate your congregation or home church about family violence.
- What community programs are available to assist churches in helping survivors of family violence.

Who Should Attend?

- Clergy, religious leaders, lay persons, Sunday School Teachers, Youth Pastors, Concerned members of congregations, family violence workers or anyone who interacts with the religious community on a regular basis.

Keynote Speaker

Pastor Roger Lyman

Pastor Lyman was a Police Officer for 30 years before going into the ministry. He began his career in Detroit, Michigan in September of 1970 and served with the Detroit Police until September of 1975. In 1975 Pastor Lyman joined the Bay City Police Department and served in that department until his retirement in 2000. While on the Bay City Police Department Pastor Lyman served in the Community Policing Division becoming the second Community Police Officer in the Department's history. While in Community Policing Pastor Lyman began the Bay City Police Departments bicycle patrol, which continues today. Pastor Lyman served as School Officer and then finished his career in the Domestic Violence unit serving from 1996 until 2000 Pastor Lyman became the Assistant Pastor at Cornerstone Baptist Church in September of 2000 serving under Senior Pastor Daniel Staples.

Facilitators

Pastor Art Zehr

Pastor Zehr is a licensed minister and currently the Minister of Outreach and Evangelism at In His Presence Ministries. He attended St. Paul's Theological Seminary in Kansas City, MO and Eastern Mennonite College in Harrison, VA majoring in Biblical Concepts. He has done extensive work in mediation with teens and adults. Pastor Zehr was also the director of the Interdenominational Christian Singles Ministry in Flint, where he conducted mediation counseling and chaired weekly programs. In this capacity he was able to be effective in counseling abused men and women. Pastor Zehr's desire is to be a liaison between the church and the community, showing that the two can work together regardless of denomination or religious affiliation.

Amy Hendrix

Amy Hendrix became the Director of the CAN Council in October 2000. Amy moved to Michigan in May 1999 from the Indianapolis area were she was the Director of a foster care and adoption agency. She earned a Bachelor's Degree in education from Ball State and a Masters Degree in Educational Psychology from Indiana University. Amy lives in Bay City and has found it to be the most philanthropic community in which she has ever lived.

Did you know that...

- **Domestic Violence occurs in 28% of all marriages in the U.S.**

- **57% of people believe that Domestic Violence is a major problem in our society.**

- **95% of all domestic violence victims are female.**

- **About 25% of all girls and 20% of all boys will have been sexually abused by their 18th birthday.**

- **Of people that were sexually abused about four out of five were abused by someone they knew.**

- **In 25% of homes where Domestic Violence occurs child sexual abuse is also occurring.**

The seminar was a great success! Many people were helped as a result.

Salvation in Color

Richard Zehr, the bishop of Croghan Mennonite church, explained salvation in colors. My dad heard the sermon about it, took notes, and sent them to me in April of 2004. Richard was the one who went over the plan of salvation with me when I accepted Christ.

Jesus is the only way. There is only one door. I came into the team through Jesus, and I really like the colors Richard came up with to represent Jesus. Perhaps these should be the colors of our baseball uniforms!

The Colors of Jesus' Life

by Biship Richard Zehr

Green reminds us of new life and Jesus' birth (Luke 2:6,7,11)

Purple shows the royalty of Jesus announced by God at Jesus' baptism (Mark 1:9-11)

Orange and warm was Jesus' voice as he chose 12 men to be His apostles (Mark 3:13-19)

Yellow represents the sunshine brought to people's lives by the teaching and miracles of Jesus (Mark 6:34, 53-56)

Pink like a pretty heart—we remember Jesus' love for us (John 3:16,1; 15:13)

Red tells of Jesus' blood and death on a cross for our sins (John 19:1-3,16-18,28-30)

Black was the sky when Jesus was buried in a tomb (Matthew 27:45,57-60)

White were the clothes of the angel who announced, "He is not here, he is risen, just as he said" (Matthew 28:2-6)

There are more colors with God than black and white. God created all the colors for whosoever. I knew Jesus likes red. But I used to think just in black and white. How did that work for me?

124

Not too well. I now like pink best. Please don't judge. I hope that this pink thing is a home run for you too. It was for me.

We come in all different colors—different colors of personalities, different colors of attitudes, different colors of backgrounds. There is no standard look or manner or personality or behavior that we can call Christian. Jesus Christ calls us in our uniqueness. The Gospel is the best of news for everyone. Author Bruce Larson says, "Whatever intellect or emotional make up or theological persuasion or philosophy or station in life, if we can understand what God has done and what He offers in Jesus Christ, we would dance before the Ark of the Lord as David did."

Eden

One morning recently on my way to church I was asking the Lord, "What is my role in Your Kingdom now today? Where is my Garden of Eden? Adam and Eve were given certain jobs to do in Eden. What do You want me to do today?"

As I was entering the sanctuary, I saw a girl kind of off to herself. I went up to her and introduced myself and lo and behold her name was Eden! I asked her, "Are you new here?"

"No, I've been here eight or ten times."

"How did you hear about us?"

"Mother sent me. She said this was a tremendous church with drama and theater." Our church has around 5,100 members. It can be overwhelming for a new person, so I grabbed the people in charge of drama, theater, young adults, etc., and introduced them to her. I connected her like a general manager. Doing so helped her to be able to belong to the team and begin expressing her gifts and graces in God's Kingdom church. She was very grateful and now greets me with a smile.

God has His unique sense of humor and He connects us. This helped me rediscover that I am a connector. Hundreds of people go to church to minister and hundreds come to be

ministered to. Some just come because they need to connect. Others need to be facilitators and mediators to help make those connections happen.

My road since the dream was great for eight years, but then it got a little rocky again. I resigned from the ministry twice more. The first time was when I was doing the singles ministry, some pastoring, and going to the seminary of that denomination. I was getting burned out and was having trouble stomaching the relativism they were teaching me at the seminary. Also there was trouble in my personal life. Finally, I told them I couldn't take it anymore. I walked out in emotional distress. This time, though, I told the Lord it wouldn't take me more than two weeks to find another church to attend. And I stuck to that promise. So, I thought I was learning better how to react to a bad situation.

The last time was after I had been plugged in to another church in Michigan (a nondenominational one this time) for a couple years, doing ministry there, but with my license still under my original denomination. There were three weddings coming up at this nondenominational church that I had been asked by the couples to preside over.

I was on a visit in my hometown when I finally asked the question that had been burning in my heart for several decades by then. "Dad, why didn't they take me on at the church up here and why don't I ever get asked to preach in this area?" My dad proceeded to tell me the whole truth, none of which I had heard before. No one had told me anything about it. I found out that practically the whole community knew about it, but me. I was completely overwhelmed with shock and disbelief and felt the pain of betrayal piercing deep into my soul.

When I returned to Michigan, I was so emotionally distraught that I could not go on. I was so disillusioned that I was done with ministry altogether. I called the three brides and explained to them that I was very sorry, but I couldn't do their weddings. The one bride pleaded with me not to cancel. I explained to her that I had finally found out what had happened about 40 years ago; that even though I had been ministering in her church, my license was with the other organization. I told her, "I am no longer going to renew my license under them. So, I can't legally do your wedding. You call Pastor Joseph and ask him what to do."

Always before I had tried to deal with ministry rejection with my own intellect, but had never dealt with my root issues. It takes the Holy Spirit to get to true, deep healing. I cried all day while spending time with the Lord. I told the Lord I wasn't going to answer any phone calls. I was just going to be alone with Him. I told Him, "God, I'm going to lay ministry on the altar. I'm not going back into it unless You resurrect it. But I'm going to keep attending church. I'm not going to miss even two weeks this time." Suddenly the phone rang. I said, "Lord, I'm not going to answer the phone."

He said, "Just look who it is." It was Pastor Joseph.

"What's going on, Art?" I told him what I had just found out about—things that ministry leaders hadn't followed through on.

I said, "I can't trust anybody anymore, not even myself. I hadn't been careful in choosing my inner circle—I didn't have a chance there!"

He ministered to me on the phone. After letting me talk out my hurt in a healing way, listening to me, comforting me, and praying with me, he asked me a poignant question. "Art, do you think ministry could've been your Isaac?" I was stunned. He was right! Ministry was the dearest, most precious thing to me. Suddenly the floodgates of my emotions came wide open. He had touched the exact right spot that released them. He then prayed over me as I gave up my "Isaac". That was a defining moment. Now, the momentum of the game was changing. The momentum of God is His Spirit.

Pastor Joseph told me he was going to go talk to Bishop Loren Covarrubias and get back to me. (Bishop Covarrubias wrote in 1994 in his book, *About Father's House,* the part of our human nature that derives satisfaction from feeling like *we have arrived* is our greatest hindrance.") Pastor Joseph called later that same day and told me, "We're not putting you on our staff, but we have no doubt that God brought you here that first Sunday in 2010. We know God has called you into ministry. We are willing to put you under our umbrella.

"Right now, you will call that bride. She called us in tears. We know all that you did for her and her fiancé. You will call her and tell her you will do her wedding." So, I did, and later I also called the other two couples.

Bishop Covarrubias also wrote about grace in *About the Father's House,* "Our gifts come from His grace at work in our lives, but our reward is determined by the development of the fruit of the Spirit in us. ... [The] bottom line [of grace] is that nothing is so evil that it can go beyond God's ability to refashion, reshape, recycle, and redirect it for His purposes."

I moved A-Z Ministries to be under their umbrella—Mt. Zion, a church of 5,100 members. The Lord got me back into ministry almost immediately after I laid my "Isaac" down. I have been focused mostly on evangelistic work since then.

I told God that I can't go through this kind of thing again without an inner circle of friends to support me. A good inner team will cover your back and will tell you the truth about things. They will stick with you through thick and thin: when things get thick, they won't thin out. God answered me first by giving me a special friend, Gary Hayward.

Psychiatrist Dr. William Glasser states in his book published in 1965, *Reality Therapy,* "At the time any person comes for psychiatric help, he is lacking the most critical factor for fulfilling his needs, a person whom he genuinely cares about and who he feels genuinely cares about him."

When the going gets rough, how many people do you know who will take the time out of their busy schedules to listen to you? How many of them would you want to know about your personal problems? Answer these questions and get a reading on the true status of your relationships: on who would come through with an emotional commitment.

Everybody needs somebody sometime. Popular people can be lonely even when they are friendly, talented, and full of the charisma that attracts others. We all need true friends! They do not change our situation or our burdens, but we then have reasons to go on! What we really crave is someone listening and understanding.

We want someone to say, "I'm sorry it is so hard." We want someone to show us they genuinely care about us and want us to get better! There are five ways I desired someone to treat me, and my friend Gary has done all of them. I'm sure you desire them too.

1. **First you want others to encourage you.** There is no better exercise for strengthening the heart and reaching down and lifting people up. Think about it. Most of your best friends are those who encourage you. You don't have many strong relationships with people who put you down. You avoid these people and seek out those who believe in you and lift you up.

2. **You want others to appreciate you.** William James, a pioneering American psychologist and philosopher in the late 1800s, said, "The deepest principle in human nature is the craving to be appreciated." Treat others as you want them to treat you. That is Jesus' golden rule. Treat them as if they are important. They will respond according to the way that you treat them. Most of us think wonderful things about people, but they never know it. We tend to be too

tight-lipped with our praise. It's of no value if all you do is think it. It becomes valuable when you impart it.

3. **You want others to forgive you.** Almost all emotional problems and stress come from unresolved conflicts—failure to have developed right relationships with people. Because of this, many people have a deep desire for total forgiveness. A forgiving spirit is the one basic necessary ingredient in a solid relationship. Forgiveness from others frees us from guilt and allows us to interact positively with people again. TWO GREAT MARKS OF A CHRISTIAN ARE THAT THEY ARE GIVING AND FORGIVING. Show me a person who walks with God, and I'll show you a person who has a giving heart and is forgiving of others.

   Too often people wait too long to forgive other people. Forgiveness should be given as quickly and as totally as possible. Do it now!

4. **You want others to listen to you.** Listening is wanting to hear. As people gain more authority, they often develop a lack of patience in listening to those under them. A deaf ear is the first indication of a closed mind. The higher people go in management and the more authority they wield, the less they are forced to listen to others. Yet their need to listen is greater than ever. The farther they get from the firing line, the more they have to depend on others for correct information, If they haven't formed the habit of listening—carefully and intelligently—they aren't going to get the facts they need, and people will resent their decisions. So learn to listen now before you are in that position!

5. **You want others to understand you.** In life you are either going to see people as your adversaries or as your assets. If they are adversaries, you will be continually sparring with them, trying to defend your position. If you see people as assets, you will help them see their potential, and you will become allies with them, making the most of each other. The happiest day of your life will be the day when you realize "we" really is the most important word in the English language.

John Lavater, who lived 250 years ago, described a good conversationalist as someone who "carefully listens, pointedly asks, calmly speaks, coolly answers, and ceases when he has no more to say." Gary is that person to me! He isn't perfect, however, he isn't controlling or judgmental. He doesn't make decisions for me! He sometimes asks me to judge myself by asking, "How is that working for you?" He encourages and supports me in my choices.

Here's a story that illustrates what kind of friend we should be.

Two Frogs

A group of frogs were traveling through the woods, and two of them fell into a deep pit. When the other frogs saw how deep the pit was, they told the two frogs that they were as good as dead. The two frogs ignored the comments and tried to jump up out of the pit with all their might. The other frogs kept telling them to stop, that they were wasting their effort, and were as good as dead. Finally, one of the frogs took heed to what the other frogs were saying and gave up. Exhausted, he quietly resolved himself to his fate, lay down at the bottom of the pit, and died.

The other frog continued to jump as hard as he could. Once again, the crowd of frogs yelled at him to stop the pain and just die. The weary frog jumped even harder and, wonder of wonders, finally leaped so high that he sprang from the pit. When he got out, the other frogs said, "Did you not hear us?" The astonished frog explained to them that he was partially deaf, and as he saw their gestures and heard their muffled shouting, he thought they were cheering him on. What he had perceived as encouragement, inspired him to try harder and to succeed against all odds.

Young Upcoming Allstars

I can't tell you about my wonderful friend Gary without telling you about his two sons. The boy on the front cover is his son Michael at just five years old. Now at age nine, he is a wonderful young man. I have watched him grow and we have been the best of friends. I think the world of him. How he did his assignment in school one day reveals what he thinks of me. I'm not sure he was quite understanding what a saint is. I will let him tell you about it himself:

> I had an assignment in 3rd grade to think of someone who acted and was like a saint. I chose Uncle Art. I wrote his name down on a blue ribbon (the kind you get for coming in first place). I chose him because he is loving and kind to everyone, and he helps lots of people with growing in faith. I mailed the blue ribbon to him. He is a really good example of loving Jesus and His people. Uncle Art is a saint!
>
> Michael Hayward
> 3rd grade, St Robert School
> Flushing, Michigan

Gary has another son who is adopted. His name is Robby. Gary's wife tells the story of how God brought Robby into their family.

> Art has been friends with my husband Gary for a very long time. I met Art just before he introduced me to Gary, fifteen years ago. I've always known Art was passionate about the Lord, but

was personally convinced of the power of his prayers a couple years ago. I confessed to him that my heart ached to have another child in my family, but I didn't want a baby. When Art confirmed with Gary and Michael that this was their desire as well, Art began to pray. Nine months later 7 year old Robby joined our family without our ever contacting an adoption agency. I just wish Art would have remembered to tell us that we were beyond "wanting" and that we were "expecting"!!

Lisa Hayward
Michael and Robby's Mom
Flushing, Michigan
2012

I have given Robby the nickname, "Mercy," because he has been adopted into this family, just as we have been adopted into God's family: by His grace and mercy. Robby really likes the nickname. I call Michael "Justice." These two fine nine-year-olds both love the Lord. I am proud of them. They both want to live their whole lives for Him. They are both hoping to become allstars on God's Kingdom baseball team.

In baseball it's all about scoring. We can't just get people on base, we must get them home. We must have fruitfulness in our lives. God the Father is waiting for the precious fruit of His

Kingdom church. We need to satisfy His desire to see His people bring forth fruit. New wine is the product of the fruit of His vine, or the wine of the church, each member of the body of Christ being a branch.

Fruitful people under pressure will draw from the power of God and begin to pour forth new wine. However, unfruitful people under pressure have nothing to pour forth and so will not be preserved. When Jesus faced the pressures of His life, He poured out Life and healing to all nations. This is exactly what the Father has purposed for each of us: His eternal purposes fulfilled in fruitfulness. God's Spirit and attitude in us is the bottom line.

We may not always see the results of our labor, but we will see the results of God's faithfulness.

We need to be planted with purpose in the diamond of Life, kept free of weeds, open to change, flexible enough to handle God's pouring forth of any pitch. We need to make sure we are not preferring our own man-made structures to moving with God. We need to understand the difference between what I am supposed to do and what only God Himself can do. An overemphasis in either direction will lead to the loss of the full blessings of God. The plate is 17 inches wide. We need balance. God is the best pitcher that ever pitched. God commands (or works) both sides of the plate. I intend to be a flexible structure, one that will fully adapt to and accommodate the movement of God's pitches, and of the wind of His Spirit.

When Jesus, the author and finisher of our faith, came to earth, He came as one with a message. However, the real message was not just what He spoke, but rather the harmony of that Word and the way He lived.

Baseball is a game of inches. Are we faithful in the little things? God will reward us with greater things. Little by little, the Word of God worked in me and through me (Ephesians 3:20).

The seal of our ministry is the fruit we produce. We must be aware that God not only watches the big things we do, but also the small things. Often those seemingly insignificant things we feel are unimportant, to God are the very things He uses to judge our hearts.

We can know the purposes and plans of God for our lives by the power of the Holy Spirit within us. We need to allow God to open our eyes to the hope of His calling and to the riches of the glory of Christ's inheritance in the saints.

God knows we will make it with His help. I may not be everything that people want me to be, but I must believe that I can be everything God wants me to be.

I continue to grow in the Lord. I have found that no matter who you are, God is going to stretch you. I had thought that once I was a pastor that I wasn't going to have any problems. I had fought so hard to do well in the ministry that God had called me to, but in the process I was hurting people, especially my family. We just weren't on the same page. We were hurting each other. I needed to apologize and try to make that right, which I did. I also needed to get over what had happened at Lockport, which took me a long time because I had always wanted to go back there. It had been the best moment in my life. I had always thought I had failed there. But I finally heard God on it. He says, "No, you were the transition guy. You did your time there." He let me know that He was the one who had closed that door.

I've learned a few things over the years from other ministers. I asked one retiring bishop what advice he had as I was taking over his position. He said, "Comfort the afflicted and afflict the comfortable." This is humorous, but there is good advice in it too.

Another bishop always said, "We will all be tried and tested all the time. We are always either going into the furnace; are in it now; or are coming out of it. So relax. You've got that to look forward to."

I've also learned some things from the mediation work I've done over the years. I used to try to convince and sell. But I found out that isn't God's style. God's style is grace. I've found that all I need to do is to just keep stating and restating the facts and keep on asking pertinent questions until the truth comes out. Then reconciliation can happen.

$\mathcal{D}$r. Frans M. J. Brandt, my special, professional mentor and friend who has written ten books, says, "Most of us, most of the time, have choices on most things." The one thing we don't have a choice about is where we are born and who our parents are. But we do have the choice to be thankful about it. I'm thankful I had God-fearing parents who were faithful to each other and reached  their 50th wedding anniversary (pictured above). And I didn't used to be, but now I'm also glad I was born Mennonite. I learned from them and from my parents about peace and loving. I learned grace from the United Methodists, and the freedom and flow of the Holy Spirit from the nondenominationals.

$\mathcal{D}$r. Brandt also says "Excellence can be attained if we are committed to: truth, reason, and faith, and [being] willing to get up, one more time, every time." In his book, *The Power of Winning Thinking,* he says, "Don't dwell on the problem, but focus on the solution," and "Winning or losing in life is more a matter of our attitudes than anything else."

Val Littfin, one of my congregants, wrote this and sent it to me:

> As I meditate on growing in my Christian life, I see baseball. My sinful self, on bad days, doesn't even put me to first base! I strike out time after time after time! Frustration sets in. I'm up to bat and I can't help the team. I can't even make it to first!
>
> Then the Spirit softly, lovingly speaks to me. The gentle, loving Lord tells me I've hit a home run! That beautiful, glorious grand slam is the fact that I am saved! Through God's grace this wonderful home run of salvation is mine!
>
> The Spirit reminds me we grow in our Christian life. We start as children—as T-ball and Little League players of Christ.
>
> We develop into strong adults and play college ball, semi-pro, and maybe even the big time. As we further mature, we are able to share our wisdom and experience with the young men and children. We are now playing slow-pitch. We know the game—the rules—the ins and outs! We are still able to enjoy the effects of the home run!
>
> Our growth in Christ is like baseball, the rules are always the same, but the skill level will change. However, a home run is still a home run!

The Final Victory

Let's start hitting more home runs! Let's start living in the victory the Lord won for us! Every serious baseball player wants to be on the winning team, but, obviously, this is not always possible. How wonderful that in the "diamond of grace" the odds are stacked completely in our favor. Jesus has won for us the most important victory of all victories, the final victory.

Dr. Brandt rightly emphasizes the urgency of the NOW when it comes to choosing a victorious life.

Human beings can indeed do marvelous things. They can be overcomers in many areas of life, but the final victory is a purely spiritual one. Victory over sin, death and the grave, come not from self-sufficiency, but are a gift from God. There is no final triumph without the selfless love of God and the power of the resurrected Christ. To be an overcomer involves choices. And, as the Scriptures so aptly point out, now is the time to choose and decide. Now is the time to tackle our self-defeating cognitions, to overcome our emotional struggles, to stand up against the powers of darkness, and to claim victory in Christ.

Quoted by permission from *The Consistent Overcomer* by Dr. Frans Brandt, WinePress Publishing, 2000, pp. 178-179.

I completely agree with Dr. Brandt that "now is the time to put the past behind us and to press on toward excellence. That, indeed, there is no better time than this very moment to choose wisely and to love God and others ... that now is the time to be an overcomer in Christ." An overcomer soon grows into maturity and fruitfulness.

Mt. Zion Church. My ministry is under their umbrella.

New Phase

So, I now belong to Mt. Zion in Clarkston, MI., and A-Z Ministry is under their umbrella. On January 1, 2012, I relaunched the third phase of my ministry. We as a church went through a period of consecration. During that period, I chose to die to self, believing God would raise me out of the ashes.

I am no longer a baby or a child. And I no longer want to be just a son. I now desire to be a mature son in whom God's Spirit can produce fruitfulness. Acts 17:28 *It is in Him I live and move and have my being.*

In our church, we are entering a new era. How exciting to hear and follow the Spirit! So that I could hear and follow better, I had to die better! Here is how I choose to die.

DYING TO SELF

Bethany Publishing House Tract

When you are forgotten or neglected or purposely set at naught, and you don't sting and hurt with the insult or the oversight, but your heart is happy, being counted worthy to suffer for Christ, THAT IS DYING TO SELF.

When your good is evil spoken of, when your wishes are crossed, your advice disregarded, your opinions ridiculed, and you refuse to let anger rise in your heart, or even defend yourself, but take it all in patient, loving silence, THAT IS DYING TO SELF.

When you are content with any food, any raiment, any climate, any society, any solitude, any interruption by the will of God, THAT IS DYING TO SELF.

When you lovingly and patiently bear any disorder, any irregularity, any impuctuality or any annoyance, THAT IS DYING TO SELF.

When you never care to refer to yourself in conversation, or record your own good works, or itch after commendation, when you truly love to be unknown, THAT IS DYING TO SELF.

When you can see your brother prosper and have his needs met, and can honestly rejoice with him in spirit and feel no envy nor question God, though your own needs are far greater and you are in desperate circumstances, THAT IS DYING TO SELF.

When you can receive correction and reproof from someone of less stature than yourself, and can humbly submit inwardly as well as outwardly, finding no resentment or rebellion rising up in your heart, THAT IS DYING TO SELF.

Are you DEAD Yet?

Truly "dying to self" is never easy, but Jesus reminded us that "death to self" leads to new life for many others (John 12:24).

As a symbol of dying to myself, I got rebaptized.

In my dying to self, God is already bringing forth fruit. Many years ago, actually about 26 years, God had made it clear that He wanted me to write—to put this sermon in a book. I knew He wasn't going to fully relaunch me until I did that, and I knew I would become whole in writing. But I hated writing and I can't spell worth beans. In all my schooling years, I would never slow down enough to write. I never wrote more than two pages at once. Writing was my Nineveh. Just as Jonah refused to go to Nineveh, I was refusing to write.

One day a friend told me, "Art, you're not going to be whole until you write. This is rebellion." That shook me up. Then later I heard a sermon preached about the disciples going fishing after the crucifixion and not catching anything. Then when the Lord told them to cast the net on the other side and they obeyed Him, they caught 153 fish.

God asked me, "Art, are you going to obey me so you can reap a harvest?"

I said, "Okay, God. I submit."

So I submitted to writing the book and thought that was over. But then God asked me to include a story that I did not want to include. So, I had to die to self and submit again. It is about one of my most embarrassing moments. It is one of my worst, infamous achievements or exploits that I will always have to live with.

Every few years Carlton and I go to Virginia to hunt with Francis and a few of his local friends. This particular year, my son was coming along for the first time. He had never hunted or even shot a gun before. My nephew was also joining us. That morning as we went out before light, I asked if anyone wanted to pray before we start. Only my son and nephew wanted to pray. The others all laughed at us. But we prayed anyway and then we were the only three who got deer that day! I was feeling very good about how God had manifested answers to our prayers!

My son had asked me to pray specifically for three things: big, buck, close. God answered with a six-point buck that he shot right under the tree. My nephew got one twenty minutes later. They were coming to me to celebrate and chased one right to me and I shot it. Francis said, "There is a God of miracles and even a blind squirrel gets an acorn once in awhile."

Well, I got excited as I was helping to gut and clean the deer in the snow on the side of a hill. I was moving too fast and slipped and landed on the antlers of the deer, cutting my leg. The huge gash started bleeding profusely. Francis and my son rushed me to the hospital, driving the windy roads as fast as they could. I was losing so much blood that they were worried I would faint. They were afraid the antler had hit an artery or something. Francis called ahead and told them he was bringing in a hunting accident victim. Well, the hospital personnel assumed I had gotten shot, so they prepared for a major trauma.

The trauma staff met me with a stretcher. As they wheeled me in, they asked, "What happened? Did the deer attack you?"

"No, no. The deer was dead." So not only was I not shot, as they thought, I wasn't even hurt by a live deer!

Well, the doctor in charge was upset! This was embarrassing to him because he had put this on number one priority! He said, "Never in this hospital have we ever treated anyone hurt by a deer, and definitely not by a dead one!"

I was extremely embarrassed. I didn't want anyone to find out about it. I just wanted to get out of there and forget the whole thing. As they were cleansing the wound and bandaging me up, my thoughts were just racing. "God, You just answered our prayers so marvelously and now this!! How in the world are You going to turn this around for good?"

The doctor had to give me two rabies shots in my hinder, as deer antlers are dangerous for that. Instead of ordering the nurse to do it, he gave me those shots himself. I think it was to take out his frustrations on me. Boy, did they hurt! Then he said, "I'm leaving you now, Mr. Zehr. My nurse will take care of the rest." I was still trying to figure out how this could ever turn out to any good, and then I saw her!

When she walked in and Francis saw my face, he knew I was going to be all right. She finished up giving me my crutches and all the bandage-changing instructions, etc. Then she asked, "Mr. Zehr, is there anything else I can do for you before you leave?"

"Yes, there is. Would you ride with me back to Michigan to explain to my congregation what happened? You are single, right?"

"No, I'm engaged, but I will tell my fiancé the story. He'll get a real kick out of it."

Strike two.

I didn't tell my congregation for two months. I was on crutches and they kept asking what happened. I told them, "It is the most embarrassing thing ever and I'm just not ready to share it. How God is ever going to turn this to good, I have no idea. I'll let you know when I'm ready to talk about it." They were in so much suspense that when I announced I would tell the story in my next sermon, they invited their friends and neighbors! The church was packed!

I didn't go back to Virginia for six years. I just couldn't bear to face the humiliation. I knew my brothers would never leave me alone. Sure enough, Francis brought a bunch of yellow ribbon. He said, "I will carry this ribbon with me, and I won't let you within 40 yards of any deer we get."

Now, every time I go they tease me. Francis introduces me, "This is my brother, Johnny the Baptist. The only difference between him and John the Baptist is his diet. John the Baptist ate only locusts and wild honey. Art eats anything in the woods. Now go get him something, but don't let him near it. Here's the yellow ribbon."

I have been able to use this story in counseling. One guy had a lot going on in his life and he was getting very depressed and discouraged about it. He called me and wanted me to counsel him. He lived quite a ways away, so I said I would meet him half way.

"What will it cost me?"

143

"A meal." So, while we ate, I shared this deer story. His look of despair soon changed. He soon began laughing out loud! So I really hammed it up and he laughed and laughed.

After he got home, he called me, "Art, I never told you my story!"

"Well, I said I would help you forget your troubles, didn't I?"

"Yes, you did."

"Did you forget?"

"You know, I haven't thought about it for two hours!" He wanted to meet with me again so he could tell me his story. I said I would as long as I got another meal out of it! He says he tells my story everywhere now to get people to laugh.

Well, I've shared my flaws and my scars. I am no longer ashamed. God can use any part of our lives for His glory. Showing our scars helps us heal and it helps other people feel free to talk about theirs.

> Scars are healed wounds. Yet, if you've been broken and barren and are still embarrassed, if you have a situation in your life that still troubles or still hurts you, ...if you still experience shame and find it difficult to talk about what happened, if the enemy still torments your mind about what God has already forgiven, if you can't seem to forgive yourself, we will help you. It's time that your misery be used as ministry to set the captives free.
>
> From the newsletter of Evangel Christian Churches, Roseville, MI.

If any of the above is true for you, first get down on your knees and ask God to heal your wounds. Then ask God to lead you to someone who can minister to you. Feel free to contact me. I have experience in inner healing ministry. My contact information is in the back of this book.

My friend, Dr. Brandt, says all counsel comes from God, but nothing changes until we self-counsel ourselves differently. We must take the responsibility to do that with the Lord's help. He shows us who He is and who we are in Him and heals us and gives us the confidence we need to turn our scars into ministry to the hurting. Out of our embarrassment, weakness, and humility comes blessings when we are healed and can laugh at ourselves. In life we always have the pitches of trials, testings, and temptations to adjust to and to hit in faith. As the bishop said, "We are either in the furnace of affliction, going in, or coming out." God is always having pitches come our way to hone and develop the gifts and graces He has given us.

"The idea that pain, disease, and heartache are not meant for God's people is total rubbish and a very cruel notion to a person who is going through those things," says Nelson, pastor of the 4,000 member Denton Bible Church in Denton, Texas. "In the day of adversity, consider, God made the one as well as the other. God creates good and calamity. He is the author ... He allows it to happen and He has a purpose for it."

"Ask great men why they are great," says Nelson. "It is not [because of] the blessings that happened to them; it is the tough times. Trials always have a beneficial purpose. They purify us and show us who we really are. They bring us to the end of our physical and intellectual rope. Trials force us to trust Christ."

... "Don't think of yourself as the smartest guy out there," Nelson quips, "because there's an outside chance you may not understand everything that's happening! We tend to think that if we can't figure it out, it must be wrong. But Solomon says, 'You're not that smart.' God has rigged life so that we have to trust Him even though it doesn't always make sense."

Not only does Solomon insist that we must trust God in the valley of the shadow of death, but also that we should enjoy life along the way! Seven times in Ecclesiastes he exhorts people to have a good time, even amid life's problems.

... "You've got to enjoy life right now!" Nelson says. "And you can't let what you can't control destroy what you can enjoy."

Creston Mapes, "Pain, Trials and the Art of Living," *In Touch* magazine, March 2003, reviewing Tommy Nelson's book, *The Problem of Life with God: Living with a Perfect God in an Imperfect World,* Broadman & Holman Publishers, 2002.

I know now that I need to stay within the laws and rules of the game laid down in the Word that God has placed within my heart by His Spirit. I need to stay under control with a renewed mind and now healthy emotions. The Holy Spirit is now controlling me instead of my emotions controlling me.

Now I know that I do not need to do it all. I can take the pressure off myself and have the joy of the Lord. Let's enjoy the game of life! Let's have fun! We have an awesome owner and manager in God! We will win!

We will make mistakes but because of God, we will win. I am no longer looking for a perfect church because people go to church. I also no longer expect perfection from myself. I love this prayer that has been floating around ever since e-mail was invented.

"Dear Lord, so far today, I've done alright. I haven't gossiped, haven't lost my temper, haven't been greedy, grumpy, nasty, selfish, or over-indulgent, but in a few minutes, Lord, I'm going to get out of bed! And from then on, I'm probably going to need a lot more help! Amen.

When the enemy approaches us with our past sins and mistakes and holds them up to our faces in taunting ridicule condemnation, recall that the Spirit says quietly and firmly, "The Father has forgiven that and has forgotten it."

Spiritual Exercise:

Every morning now I do my spiritual stretching exercises to warm up for the day. My friend, Dr. Frans M. J. Brandt put together this card, "Steps to Spiritual Fitness," that I use for my daily spiritual exercise routine. It has become very precious to me. I carry this card with me everywhere I go.

STEPS TO SPIRITUAL FITNESS

LIVE BY THE LOVE OF GOD

A Christian's spiritual fitness is firmly founded on faith in Christ and salvation by grace (Eph. 2:8), but is *SOLELY* manifested by fruits. Words (however eloquent), appearances (however impressive), memberships (however desirable), roots (however important), or dogma (however convincing), do *not* determine spiritual fitness. The latter must be unequivocably manifested in our life, by acts of love toward God and others (Mark 12:29-31), and a readiness to lay down our life for those we profess to love (John 15:13). The "Steps to Spiritual Fitness" only highlight some important aspects of a disciplined walk with our Heavenly Father by sharing him in LOVE, DISCIPLESHIP, FELLOWSHIP, STEWARDSHIP, and WORSHIP. A walk (thoughts, feelings, actions) motivated by the LOVE of GOD: forgiving, generous, hopeful, humble, kind, modest, patient, peaceful, persevering, protective, trusting, truthful, unselfish, and unwavering (1 Cor. 13:2; 4-8). We are to live gracefully and gratefully (Col. 3:12-17) by the love of God.

LIVE BY THE VOICE OF GOD

As we read the *Word of God* we learn to listen to the *Voice of God*. A God of love: Knowledge and wisdom, faith and reason, justice and mercy, holiness and righteousness. Always remember there is only ONE *godhead* (Mat. 3:16-17); *God* (Deut. 4:35), *Christ* (Rom. 1:4) *Holy Spirit* (John 15:26); *kind of human being* (Rom. 3:10); *redeemer* (Eph. 1-7), *salvation* (Acts 4:12); *mediator* (1 Tim. 2:5), *moral standard* (Gal. 5:24); *aspiration* (Phil. 3:13-15); *death* (Heb. 9:27), and *final judgment* (Rev. 20:12). "... and his sheep follow him because they know his voice (John 10:4). We are to *faithfully study* the Word of God.

LIVE BY THE WILL OF GOD

It is God's desire that we turn away from sin and be saved by the blood of Christ. Basic to spiritual fitness is an *acknowledgment of sin* (Luke 18:13), *repentance* (Acts 3:19), *confession* (1 John 1:9), *faith in Christ* (John 3:16) and a *willingness toward baptism* (Acts 2:38). God also desires that we continually communicate with him through PRAYER (1 Thes. 5:7). This is as essential for spiritual empowerment, as is a steadfast and unwavering FAITH. We must share our spiritual abundance with others, confess Christ and be witnesses of his love in all we say and do. This also includes, following the example and teachings of Christ (Mat. 3:13-16; Mark 16:16), incorporation into the body of Christ through baptism.

Back:

Sonship of Christ also entails union with him in his suffering. This enables us to partake of his glory (Rom. 8:16-18), and to become "pillars in the temple of God." (Rev. 3:12). It is the will of God that we trust and obey him. He has a sovereign will (Eph. 1;11), and a general moral will (Rom. 2:18). Only through obedience can we accept God's authority and do his will (Deut. 11:26-28; John 14:15,21). Those who are hearers of the Word, but not doers, deceive primarily themselves (James 1:22). Spiritual fitness demands a yielding of our imperfect will to the perfect will of God; this leads to blessings and joy. Perfect obedience to God equals perfect happiness in God. We are to trust and obey.

LIVE BY THE SPIRIT OF GOD

Spiritual fitness refers to the quality or power by which a believer incorporates and manifests God's Holy Spirit with such attributes as love, forgiveness, justice, kindness, mercy, faith, prayer, righteousness, steadfastness, unselfishness and virtue (Gal. 5; Eph. 5). Believers *must* pattern their love and forgiveness after God (Eph. 4:32) to love unconditionally (seek only good and no harm for others), and to forgive those offending fellow-believers they have confronted and who have repented (Luke 17:3). Yet, many of the consequences of sin (e.g., legal, marital, financial, physical) may well remain. The Scriptures teach three kinds of forgiveness:
1. *Legal forgiveness* found in salvation by grace through the atoning sacrifice of our Lord and Savior Jesus Christ (John 3:16; 1 John 2:1-2).
2. *Family forgiveness* which is accorded by God (Eph. 2:19) to those who have legal forgiveness, if new sins are confessed (1 John 1:9).
3. *Interpersonal forgiveness* which is obtained between fellow-believers upon reproof and repentance (study Mat. 6:14-15;18:15-17,23-25; Luke 3:8; 17:3; Acts 26:20; Rom. 12:19-21). If we are to live by the Spirit of God we must pattern our forgiveness after God.

LIVE BY THE MIND OF GOD

Spiritual fitness requires the removal of old sinful character traits and their replacement with new Christian traits such as patience, honesty, integrity, faithfulness, humility, purity, devotion, moderation and so forth. God wants us to be victorious over *depraved* (Rom. 1:28-32), *blinded* (2 Cor. 4:3-4), *unclean* (Mark 7:20-23), *vain* (Eph 4:17), *doubtful* (James1:5-8), and *carnal* (Rom. 8:5-8) *minds!* Believers are to have a renewed mind, the mind of Christ; one of goodness, truth, and righteousness (Eph. 5:9). The mind of God is the mind of Christ within us (Luke 17:21; Col. 1:27). Spiritual fitness demands that we give executive control of our mind to Christ, in order to have a life of joy, righteousness and true holiness (Eph. 4:22-24); hid with Christ in God! All our actions are in vain without the love of God (1 Cor. 13). We are to have a mind of love in order to be renewed and transformed.

Today there is a lot of emphasis put on *physical* fitness. The Bible says "bodily exercise profits a little. but godliness is profitable for all things" (1 Tim. 4:8). So it is more beneficial for us to have a daily *spiritual* exercise regimen than it is to go to the gym regularly. I am honored that Dr. Brandt gave me permission to reproduce his tested and proven spiritual fitness program.

I have come to the conclusion that it isn't about me. I am learning not to be so focused on seeking God's "Atta boy!" I now want to focus my attention on the awesomeness of God and on giving Him praise—giving Him an "Atta God!"

In the past I was diminished by others perception of me and my own definition of myself. Now I know that to live by grace means to acknowledge my whole life story, the light side and the dark. In admitting my shadow side, I learn who I am and what Gods Grace means. As Thomas Merton puts it:

A SAINT IS NOT SOMEONE WHO IS GOOD BUT WHO EXPERIENCES THE GOODNESS OF GOD.

To this day, I still have the same desires I wrote on a slip of paper in 1961 at the age of 17:

Know Christ
Be like Christ
Tell others about Christ

Who is this Jesus Christ? Why is hope founded on Him alone? For one simple reason that has many facets. Jesus is grace!!! The simplest explanation of grace is Jesus. The Gospel of Jesus Christ is the Gospel of grace. Jesus is the foundation of the church's being. Without Christ there is no church—no you or me; without Jesus of Nazareth there is no reality for the church or for you or me. Because of His identity, because of His life and ministry, because of His atoning death and resurrection, His gift of the Holy Spirit and His promise of ultimate victory, believers are drawn into a fellowship of hope. To fail to understand Jesus Christ is to fail to understand grace or the church or our very lives.

Jesus is "Radiant Light" according to Hebrews 1:3 "being the brightness of His glory." If there is radiation, there must be a source; that is, because of the nature of Jesus we know there must be some radiating source—God's own glory. Nicodemus

could see that. "No one can do these signs that you do unless God is with him" (John 3:2). Christ is the personal manifestation of God on earth! He is the very essence of God Himself. The best picture God ever took was as a baby!

God desires a new diamond—a new family—of the redeemed—of those twice-born: of the flesh and of the Spirit. This diamond is the Kingdom of God. It was the dream in the heart of God from the foundation of the world. God envisioned a team, a remnant, in which He would be the loving Father and every member a caring, loving, productive person. The architectural plan indicated the need for a Redeemer and Christ was appointed to fulfill that role.

The team would be made up of those who responded in faith and obedience; those willing to risk the impossible and follow God out of the Egypts of their particular forms of bondage, through trackless wastes of leanness, and crossing swollen rivers to take the Promised Land, all the while believing God provides for what He has commanded.

Come to Me, all you who labor and are heavy laden, and I will give you rest (Matt. 11:18).

I pray that out of his glorious riches he may strengthen you with power through his Spirit in your inner being (Eph 3:16 NIV).

God's eternal purpose and bottom line is that we believe in and receive the Spirit and grace of Jesus Christ. Whosoever responds with a yes to believe and follow Jesus, God welcomes with an amen!!!

So be it!!! Amen!!!

GOD we thank You for Your bottom line eternal purposes of GRACE in JESUS CHRIST in the diamond of life.

HOLY SPIRIT, we humbly ask that You will give us perception and application so we can field Your faithful promises in the spirit and attitude of JESUS.

Help us to experience the JOY OF THE LORD in hitting home runs for Your KINGDOM TEAM!

TO SCHEDULE REV. ART ZEHR

FOR A SPEAKING ENGAGEMENT:

E-mail him at

az4god247@yahoo.com

THIS BOOK IS AVAILABLE AT:

olivepresspublisher.org
amazon.com
barnesandnoble.com

BOOK STORE MANAGERS may obtain this book
at wholesale, returnable through
Ingram Book Company
or through
Olive Press Publisher

by e-mailing: olivepressbooks@gmail.com

THE E-BOOK IS AVAILABLE

for only $9.95
on Kindle at
amazon.com

CPSIA information can be obtained at www.ICGtesting.com
Printed in the USA
BVOW030150231112

306217BV00005B/3/P